MW00907153

Luis Pástor

Riding the Bus with JESUS

Luis Pástor

Copyright © 2018

Luis Pástor

All rights reserved.

ISBN-13: 978-1539663560

Luis Pástor

Table of Contents

Luis Pástor

ABOUT THE AUTHOR

Mr. Luis Pástor is author of three books: Riding the Bus 1, saving money, dreams and inspiration; Riding the Bus 2, the sequel; Riding the Bus 3, the dream continues, and this series Riding the Bus with Jesus is the fourth. This fourth edition was born after the publishing of his first book. When presenting his book to a friend, this emerging poet was advised not to call himself a Christian if he was promoting his book to the secular world. Mr. Pástor looked at his friend straight in the eyes and exclaimed, "You just gave me a great idea, Riding the Bus with Jesus", thus the birth of this fourth book. Still Mr. Pástor claims that his books, especially the current one, is for everybody and anybody because Jesus came to save everybody, not just Christians.

Mr. Pástor was in the education sector for more than 30 years as a teacher aide and as a teacher of French, Spanish and ESL. He discovered writing ever since his childhood when he would write short stories with his vocabulary words both in English, French and Spanish. During the past 10 years Mr. Pástor reconnected with his passion for writing and has plans of publishing 10 books. Next to be published will be two screen plays: My Mommy is a Mummy and Return of the Bad Prince. He has published several poems in Spectrum publishing, sponsored my saturdayafternoonpoetry.com. He has participated in poetry readings at Santa Catalina Branch Library, Pasadena Central Library, Beyond Baroque, T.U. Studios and local churches. As part of his warm-up, Mr. Pástor would begin his lessons with motivational poems to inspire and to keep his students centered and on check.

Order other books published by Mr. Pástor @
Riding the Bus 1: www.createspace.com/4351776
Riding the Bus 2: www.createspace.com/4263297
Riding the Bus 3: www.createspace.com/4630433
Riding the Bus with Jesus: www.createspace.com/6662171
Thank you for your patronage. ☺

ENDORSEMENTS

Luis Villalobos is a good, kind Christian whose
devotion is expressed in his poetry.
David Stern, musician

I recommend Riding the Bus with Jesus to anyone interested in
poetry not just as fancy, flowery words but a medium to inspire
and transform lives. Mr. Villalobos' story poems bring to light
the extraordinary human spirit in seemingly ordinary life on the
bus. Through these bittersweet anecdotes, the poet persona
maintains a positive perspective which he passes to his reader--
"You have two choices in life, to be positive or to be positive."
Jackie Chou, published poet

Luis Villalobos' poetry speaks of the power found in Spirituality,
forgiveness and humility. This collection includes soothing works
such as, "Balanced Gospel" which ask
the reader every angle of "what if" words can offer
to a healing-heart-expanding-in-faith.
Beverly M. Collins, Author of Mud in Magic.

I am writing this endorsement for Luis Villalobos. I have had the
honor to get to know him and his poetry writing. He is an
empathetic and caring man ensuring that his poetry will help you
with the things going on in your life. I am glad I have been able
to get to know him and by reading his poetry it has made me a
stronger person.
Karen Williams, retired high school counselor

Mr. Villalobos is just awesome. I felt he was a teacher who
genuinely cared about the well-being of his students. Just like
being an awesome teacher I am sure he is an awesome father,
and his words of wisdom and poetry will follow his children and
his students where ever they go.
Josecarlos Lopez, former student

Thought provoking and inspiring verse for a modern stress-
filled world. Candi, from Santa Barbara, California.

Luis, the fluent French poet/author. His delivery of his subject matter is not only profound but timely as well. You want a positive lift, I encourage you to read and become a passenger on riding the bus, enjoy. James Petty

ACKNOWLEDGMENTS

I would like to thank my Lord and Savior Jesus Christ
for inspiring me to write this book. I want to thank
all my Facebook buddies, my students, colleagues,
family, extended family and friends, especially
Don King Fisher Campbell and all my
fellow poets from Saturday Afternoon
Poetry for your encouragement
and support in the journey
to make our world a
better place.

DEDICATION

I would like to dedicate
this book, first and
foremost, to my
Lord and
Savior,
Jesus Christ. Nevertheless, this book is not only
for Christians but for anyone who wants to
explore poetry and Christianity. Jesus
came to the world for everyone,
especially for those who
are looking for
something
new.

Luis Pástor

Preface

I am truly looking forward to and excited to publish of my fourth book of poetry, "Riding the Bus with Jesus." I am ashamed to admit that this is the second time I attempt this book. I was at least 80 percent finished when my computer crashed while visiting my brother in Tijuana, when someone hacked my computer and sent it into a loop. I am even more ashamed to tell you that I did not save my book on my flash drive even though I always carry one in my "lucky" fanny pack. Since I am now retired, I never dreamed that my computer would crash since I no longer store hundreds of documents belonging to the teaching profession. Well, there is always a good side to every story. Now I have the opportunity to rewrite this introduction. Fortunately, most of my book is manuscript in my composition book and the rest is in my mind, my heart and the lessons life may bring me.

Well, enough of that story. Let's talk about the purpose of this book #4 (Please look into Riding the Bus 1, 2 and 3 also by this author). "Riding the Bus with Jesus" is a transparent book. My fourth book is the place where we can look in the mirror and see ourselves as we are. There is no need to hide major events in our lives that have shaped our future. Some have been positive events, but it is the bad experiences that we want to keep secret. It is now time to admit that fate led us down the path of divorce, that we suffered unjustly at the hands of an abuser. It is ok to walk away from a bad situation or stay and fight if you so choose. But equally important, we must remember the good times too, our triumphs, our victories and be thankful for every moment, good or bad.

"Riding the Bus with Jesus" will be a collection of story poems about life. These stories are about triumph, whether terrific or tragic, they are another reason to be thankful as the apostle Paul wrote, "Be thankful for everything, for all things work together for good for those who love God." Staying positive in the face of opposition is an art that can only be learned through the lessons in life. You can look at the glass half empty or half full. You can look at what you lost or what you gained. "Riding The Bus Jesus" is a journey through life where we can discover the undiscovered, rediscover, climb the mountain and see that there are more mountains and valleys on the other side. It is an honest depiction of who I am, who I want to be, where I have been and where I am going.

I must emphasize that my experiences are not exclusive. There are millions of people who have gone through a divorce, became depressed and retired early. Many parents have had trouble with their children and some have lost their children. Many of us got in trouble or we are still in trouble because we are still spending above our limits using the greatest evil, greatest scam ever invented: credit! Perhaps we made other decision that changed the course of our lives for good or for bad. If you don't have cash, you shouldn't have it. We should all live within our means, but we don't.

My poems are not sad stories of failure, they are the reality of triumph. We all go through stuff but we shouldn't stay there. It is my earnest prayer and desire that my wife and I will reunite. Now things are looking good and God gave me an interesting revelation: I need to go back to my wife every day from here on, every day is a new beginning.

My children are doing better now, they both have jobs and depression seems to be in the past for the most part, of course like anything else, they have to keep working at it. My son is back to playing his violin, his love. My daughter has taken a different route and now she works for a law firm and wants to work in social justice. The family as a whole is better off, happier and moving forward. We just had to go through the fire. Although I talk about God in my poems, the purpose of my book is not to convert anyone to anything. It is an open window to the things I believe about God, how He helps me through the day and the wiles of life. It is not a religious source where I am going to argue the existence of God. I will not try to prove that Jesus is God or that He was only a prophet. The advocates of atheism and those who disagree have equal arguments. Today we have debates in high schools and universities that discuss everything from God to sex to social justice. If I am going to prove anything I am going to prove it to myself. The only proof I need that God exists is my refrigerator. Let me explain. Now that I am retired I experience many moments of silence where I can just stop and think. My daughter lives and works in New York, my son is off freelancing and working, my wife is spending long hours at the Food court, la "taquería" in Vallarta supermarket and I am home alone. It is at that moment when the purring of my refrigerator catches my attention, and I know God is there. That silence is the presence of God.

Let me, nevertheless, tell you a little more about what I believe and perhaps challenge you. Besides the noise of my refrigerator breaking the silence in my house I believe in Jesus because He is unique. As far as I know Jesus is the only one who died and rose from the dead (or at least the only story that has spread throughout the world this long). He is the only one who claimed to die for the sins of the world. He said He was the only way to the Father. If you can believe that The Father is the representative of the only true God then it makes sense that Jesus is the only way to God. I believe that I am a sinner, that Jesus is my Savior, that I am going to heaven and that I can live a better life here on earth with the presence of Jesus in my life. This is not a book about theology so I will not discuss whether Jesus is only the Son of God or only God. There are many arguments to that effect. My take is that such a question should not even be posed. Jesus is the Son of God, period. I don't wish to debate with the Mormons, Jehovah's Witnesses, Seventh day Adventists or the Apostolic beliefs or anyone else. I just want to share Jesus with you openly and honestly.

Highlights

I say I like all my poems but some of them have a special tone. The poem "Jazz" and the poem "The Poet Tree" took a lot of energy and effort. I was presented with two prompts: a mini jazz concert and the second, anything that came to mind. It takes a

certain amount of creativity to transform a jazz music concert into a Jesus poem and staring at a tree, I imagined a tree that was a poet. Then it became even more complicated to "Jesusize" both of these poems. Was it my imagination or God's Holy Spirit that made me think about the stripes on Jesus and the strips on a zebra? Is it possible that the very bark on a tree would testify to the horrendous crime committed against Jesus?

Two other poems that I enjoyed writing are "Why" and "The Ferrari principle". These poems question the essence of God. How do people get to the point of finally believing that there is a God. Does an individual need to hit rock bottom to turn to the hope of a God? In my case, the absence of a God makes my life meaningless. For me it is not enough to have science explain to me the elements of an atom, I need to know about the One that made the atom. Many of my poems end with open-ended questions and thoughts. I don't presume to answer the question "why", instead I want to be a guiding light and help people discover God for themselves. After spending some time with Jesus, the apostles were asked why they believed and they answered, "Only you have words of life." That's where I am today.

I said it once and I will say it again. It is difficult for me to choose which poems are my favorite because I seem to like them all, even those that I think are not very good. In my past books my readers have surprised me by telling me that their favorite poem was that very poem I thought was too bland. It is not surprising though, because people will take the same text and it will speak different things to different individuals. Li'l Job 1, 2 and 3 is a storyline that explains the three stages I went through (the third stage will continue for the remainder of my life) and others like you might undertake. But we went through it, we didn't stay there. Li'l Job 1 describes the devastation I felt when my life began to spiral downward after the fall of the economy, the divorce and my son's depression. I tried to correlate my experience with that of Job in the Bible. Li'l Job 2 is stage two where I begin to understand that I need to give all my cares to my God. Li'l Job 3 is a prediction of how God is going to restore my family. Consequently, now my wife and I are working on reestablishing our relationship and our marriage. I must repeat that God has given me a revelation that I not only need to go back to my wife, but I need to go back to her every day. Each morning is a new beginning. And I am a "little" Job because my experience does not compare to the extreme pain, abandonment and suffering of BIG Job in the Bible.

"Riding the Bus with Jesus" contains three related poems that may be controversial: The Prosperity Gospel, the Desperation Gospel and the Balanced Gospel. In several occasions I have heard pastors say that people don't want to go to church or believe because they see Christians fight and bicker amongst themselves and that turns them off. Jesus said, "By your works they will know you are my disciples." It is sad how there are so many churches that differ on the smallest of things. Small churches and large churches alike are splitting on issues that some may consider trivial. The issue of not attending church or believing in God may come from a deeper personal issue though. The fact is that we all judge and criticize each other whether in church or the supermarket. If we say there are hypocrites in the churches, there are also hypocrites in grocery stores, banks, the post office, everywhere. Unfortunately, we don't hold every establishment to the same standard. If you ever board a bus where I am riding, you will be riding with a hypocrite, because I too say things I don't do and make promises I can't keep. I am not perfect.

"Dr. Yo" and "Dr. Tú" are two comical poems that could only

come about through a miracle. It is opportunities like these that poets with creativity run to, chase and catch. I don't think it is a coincidence that two Chinese doctors with names that carry a Spanish connotation came together to restore my sight. I'd like to think that God named these doctors and made me their patient to see what I would do. I believe that God has a sense of humor. If God was going to give me 20/20 vision through science he would have to be creative like spitting on the dirt, making a ball of mud, applying it to the eye and asking his patient to go wash in the river.

Aside from my three poems regarding the scrutiny of Christians by other Christians, I have some poems that may be misconstrued as political. I say misconstrued because it is not my intent to discuss politics on the favor of the left, right, middle or independent. I approach the issue of immigration, injustice and homelessness from a moral vantage point. In my poem "The Orange Man" I want to contrast the disparity between hard labor and a white-collar job such as the President of the United States. It was too tempting not to find some correlation between the hard-working man selling oranges by the freeway and the earned nickname of President Trump. With this poem I want my readers to enter the sentiments of these men who sell on the streets with hopes of seeing a better tomorrow. It is not my intent not to create a division between supporters and non-supporters: that divide already exists. I want to create an awareness of the underdog and I hope I accomplished my attempt to be comical and entertaining. I say/joke that our country should be more united today more than ever because we have never had a president who can make both democrats and republicans laugh to their heart's desire.

Overall my poetry is about resilience. My poem "Round infinity" gives hope to an individual caught in a struggle. In Riding the Bus 3, I published a poem called round #15. It is an allusion to the Rocky movies where Silvester Stallone would fight to the end of round 15 and tie or win by a knock out. I think our life struggles are similar. If we want to win, we can win if we just keep fighting and with God on our side, we cannot lose. God will keep counting until we get up again.

There are many other poems that I could talk about but I will leave it up to the reader to be inspired in his/her own unique way. You will identify with my story/poems based on your own experience or you will relate them to friends and family. You will discover your own favorite poems and you might find that you have lived that experience or you can prepare for the inevitable. Whatever the case, it is my hope that you will be inspired and that your life will improve as you take your journey through the pages of my life.

Well, I think this paragraph should be first in my introduction. Riding the Bus with Jesus is not exclusive to Christians. It is a fallacy to say that Jesus Christ is only for Christians. Jesus when here on earth, would heal the sick, the lame, the blind... He would not give sight to the seeing. Likewise, it is my hope that my readers, Christians, atheists, non-Christians will find enjoyment, inspiration, and resolve as they leaf through my pages and my poems. Hopefully you will take a chance with Jesus, you have nothing to lose but everything to gain.

Before You Embark

My books of poetry are the type that you can pick up and put down after you read one page. All of my poems start and end on the same page. They all begin with a short back story or introduction. If you are not a strong reader, this book is perfect for you. It can be used as a devotional if you like or it can be read during your leisure time. My poems are unique in that every poem attempts to teach something. All introductions contain a reflection, message, a lesson or moral that will hopefully move the reader to engage in deep thought about life. But don't be surprised if you pick up any of my books and can't put them down as some of my readers have shared.

As you take your tour through my 104 poems you might be reminded of something that happened to you or a loved one. Feel free to write in the margins, make notes and your own reflections. Hopefully you will be challenged to take risks in your life, follow that dream you have been postponing. Perhaps presently you are in a place in your life where you want to be, if so, my poems can serve as reassurance. If not, this can be the time in your life to move forward, start that business, go back to college, get that dream girlfriend/boyfriend or give Jesus a chance, recommit your life to God or go back to your ex. No one knows better what you need than you.

Now you are ready to begin your exodus through my poems, my stories, my reflections and messages. Be ready to discover yourself and uncover yourself and expose yourself to your own future. Feel free to disagree with me, to cry, get angry, get sad and get happy, but don't throw things. ☺ Go ahead! Get hungry to learn, to grow, to go beyond your wildest dreams.

A BETTER PLACE (1)

Message: I said this once and I need to say it again. My poetry is about faith and using the power of faith to accomplish the impossible, or at least attempt it. It is not my intent to prove anything but instead, to give hope to people. I must admit, though, that my faith is in Jesus. According to history and what I think I know, Jesus is the only One who said He was dying for the whole world and He is the only One who came back to life, and I believe this by faith, that's all.

A BETTER PLACE (1)

I live in the mundane city of Monrovia,
Probably no different than your city of old,
I invite you to a better place far and beyond,
An eternal place where there is no pain or sorrow.

A man named Jesus is preparing a place,
In His Father's house beyond the stars,
He said He was the way, the truth and the life,
The way to cross over to the truth, a better place.

I'm not trying to prove anything or convince you,
After all, who really knows the truth?
But why not believe in the unsure, the invisible?
After all, the unknown is where the answer lies.

What if He really did die for our sins?
What if there really is a life after tomorrow?
I invite you to take a risk, dare to believe,
If it is not true, there is nothing to lose,

But if it is, I definitely want to be in my Savior's house.

A BURRO FOR THE LORD (2)

Reflection: For this poem I decided to use the Spanish version for the word "donkey", rather than using the King James version: ass. Although all three have negative connotations I question why God would choose a donkey to transport Mary to Bethlehem. Jesus the King of the Jews rode a donkey into Jerusalem. The prophet Balaam would not obey God until He made a donkey speak. I think the purpose of a donkey is to teach us a lesson on humility.

A BURRO FOR THE LORD (2)

If God could use a burro
to speak to the prophet Balaam,
how much more can He use you
to speak the truth to your neighbor?

If God could use a burro
to take Mary to Bethlehem,
then God can use you
to lead someone down the right path.

If Jesus could use a burro
to ride into town triumphantly,
what can God do through you?
Can you change someone for the better?

I want to be a burro for the Lord.
Don't have to be a great stallion.
In God's eyes, I am the best, and of course,
I don't want to be an ass for devil.

A FENCE (3)

Moral: Once a week I and some friends meet at Coco's
Restaurant in Covina, California for Monday night Bible study.
The title of today's lesson was "the meaning of love." Our
teacher shared that hate, unforgiveness, failure to ask for
forgiveness builds "a fence" with every "offence" that is
unforgiven. Every new unforgiven offence adds a new stake to
the separation between you, your human relationships and God!
It is important to realize that hate and regret hold back love and
life. If you want to move forward, forgive, ask for forgiveness
and embrace love.

A FENCE (3)

You lied to me, you never called me back,
You let me down, I trusted you.
But I forgive you because I love you.

Please forgive me, that's not what I meant.
It is not easy to ask for forgiveness,
A person has to be humble to admit a mistake.

If there is a fence between you and your offender,
Begin by forgiving one offence at a time,
Take down the fence that separates you.

A fence and offence rhyme for a reason,
Every offence adds one more spike,
To the white picket fence.

Learn from your Heavenly Father,
Who has erased all you've ever done,
Tear down that fence.

Ask for forgiveness, forgive and forget.
Set yourself free from hate and regret.

A SURGE OF ENERGY (4)

Message: Isaiah 40:31 says, "I shall mount up with wings like eagles, run and not get tired, walk and not faint." In life we have goals and sometimes is seems useless to keep trying when things aren't working out. As a person of faith I can't help but lift up my arms into the air, as tired as I am, and just keep going. This morning I felt defeated so I lifted my arms to the sky and prayed, "Lord, pick me up as you would pick up a pretty little baby."

A SURGE OF ENERGY (4)

Sometimes it is hard to keep going,
Obstacles in the way: financial, relational,
Feels like I am walking backwards.

I look up into the sky,
The horizon looks bleak, hopeless,
All of a sudden, a bird,
Springs from one tree to another.

Then I begin to wonder,
What lies beyond the clouds?
How does a bird pick up its wings to fly?

Suddenly, I felt a great serge,
Energy filled my bones, my flesh,
The eagle in Isaiah 40:31 came alive,
I picked up my arms in the air.

Like a bird, an eagle, I will soar through life once again.
I will chase my dreams once again,
And I won't stop until I catch them! ☺

ALL...BUT GOD... (5)

Message: In the Book of Genesis there is a story about Joseph who was sold into slavery by his brothers. About 13 years later God ascended Joseph to second in command in Egypt. The Bible says that pharaoh called ALL his magicians and diviners but no one could interpret his dreams. Word got to pharaoh that Joseph had the power to interpret dreams and his fate changed for the better when he was called out of jail. After pharaoh had exhausted ALL his resources, ONLY GOD was able to give him the answer he was looking for.

ALL...BUT GOD... (5)

"I hear you have the power
To interpret dreams." "I don't possess such a gift
BUT GOD will give you the answer."

Joseph was able to interpret pharaoh's dreams,
And he prepared Egypt for the 7-year drought.
Egypt became the supplier of grain,
For all surrounding cities and people.

Likewise, have you taken ALL medicine.
Perhaps your doctors have done ALL they could?
BUT GOD can still heal you.

God is able to do what no one else can.
God is preparing you for hard times to come.
You can become the go-to-person,
For people looking for answers?

Maybe you've tried ALL kinds of things,
BUT ALL you have to do is trust in GOD.
Give ALL your cares to GOD,
And He will see you through. ☺

ALWAYS LOADED (6)

Reflection: I have talked about my lucky pen before throughout my poems. I have been using said pen since the onset of my first student trip to Europe in 2010. It was then when I purchased my fanny pack to protect my money and credit cards from pocket pickers. Because I am eccentric I attached three elastic chains, one blue, one red, and one green. The blue chain keeps my lucky pen permanently attached to my fanny pack, ready to serve when called to duty. It has been a lender in banks, stores, post offices, the bus and more.

ALWAYS LOADED (6)

My guns are always loaded,
I don't mean to kill anyone,
I'm talking about my lucky pen,
Attached to my fanny pack with elastic.

People standing in line with straight faces,
"Excuse me sir, do you have a pen I can borrow?"
Actually, I do. I'll lend you my pen if you
Promise not to walk off with it." Laughter breaks out.

When you lend a pen to someone,
They usually take it with them,
Not because they are stealing it,
Both you and the other person forgot.

My gun is always loaded,
Ready to strike with the power of the pen,
To break out with encouraging words or a helping hand,
Ready to continue, to stretch out the dream.

But be careful, words can be deadly too,
They can cut through the heart and fix it too,
God's Word is a two-edged sword,
Like a gun or knife can kill, or save a life too.

ATTRIBUTES (7)

Reflection: While meditating on Psalms146, day 23 of "Regenerate" at Faith Community Church I stumbled upon the concept of God's attributes. In the reflection section Pastor Dawn asks the reader to meditate on God's attributes. I began to think of all that God means to me and all He has done for me. I will attempt to describe God's attributes in the following poem which will be clearly impossible. I believe His attributes are infinite.

ATTRIBUTES (7)

My savior, my redeemer, my forgiver,
My strength, my courage, protection,
My love, my provider, my future,
My eternity, my security, my assurance.

These are just a few of the attributes of God,
That have my best interest at hand,
All He wants to do is prosper me,
As He wants me to bless those around me as well.

He is all powerful, omniscient, omnipresent,
He knows what I am thinking, what I feel,
He knows what I am going to do, not going to do,
I have nothing to worry about, no need to hide.

If you want to know about God,
Read books, the Bible, the Koran,
The Book of Mormon, Confucius,
My series of "Riding the Bus,"
Search for God and you will find Him.

BALANCED GOSPEL (8)

Moral: It is sad how Christian churches criticize others. Those who listen to Christian pop music criticize those who don't for being legalistic, while those who listen to traditional hymns call the others worldly. A wise bus driver once told me that they were all wrong and I agreed. God is bigger than all that. The Bible says, "For all have sinned, and they fall short of the glory of God." Perhaps this verse denotes the state of all humans.

BALANCED GOSPEL (8)

Is the body divided?
Can the hands say to the feet?
I don't need you, you're not important.

Are the eyes more useful than the nose?
Can the head eat without a mouth?
Are some body parts more essential than others?

So, with the body of Christ,
We need pastors, preachers, evangelists,
Are the teachers, healers, custodians, less necessary?

Likewise, the formation of the earth,
Unjust balances are an abomination to the Lord,
In his hands the earth is perfectly balanced.

We need mega churches to reach the masses,
We need small churches to build close communities,
Jesus spoke to crowds but traveled with only twelve.

If you want to live a balanced life.
Don't do too much of this, a little of that,
Balance yourself through the eyes of Jesus.

BIRD OF PARADISE (9)

Reflection: Sometimes people may think that certain tasks are impossible but if you believe, the impossible becomes possible. I was determined to have my mother-in-law take my bird of paradise to her garden in Mexico. My wife and my mother-in-law warned me that the plant would not pass customs. I stripped down my bird to one flower and a small root, rapped roots in wet paper towels and sealed it in an air-tight plastic bag. My bird flew across the plains and mountains of Mexico and is flourishing to this day, in my mother-in-law's garden.

BIRD OF PARADISE (9)

Its wings spread out, its beak majestic,
In shades of red, yellow, green, and blue,
Standing on a small piece of dirt and roots.

Flying over the ocean, plains, mountains, and meadows,
It imagines his mother-in-law's beautiful paradise garden,
With exotic plants from Mexico and all the world.

There I will start a new life, new family,
My children will grow up to be proud,
Breathing in the humidity and tropical rains.

Finally, my bird lands in Guadalajara,
Quickly they rush my bird to the little town of Pihuamo,
My bird busts out of its plastic bag into paradise,
And jumps into the ground of my ancestors.

It sinks its roots deep in the soil,
And drinks to its heart's desire,
Then he reflects, "I'm glad my dad snuck me in,
If God protected him as a wetback across the Rio Grande,
Certainly, a wet bird like me can pass Mexican customs."

CAN'T SELL JESUS (10)

Reflection: As a general rule, I share with people on the bus about my published books. Most people show a lot of interest and once in a blue moon I will sell a book or two. On this occasion I met a man who was intoxicated and did not approve of my telling the bus driver that she could have my books, three for twenty dollars. He interrupted, "You can't sell Jesus, I'll kick your ass off this bus." I ignored him till I reached my stop.

CAN'T SELL JESUS (10)

"You have made my house a den of robbers!"
People selling doves, changing money, buying and selling,
The house of prayer had been defiled, now house of profit.

How do these words of Jesus relate to today's Church?
All churches buy and sell, hold fundraisers,
They sell books, CDs, coffee, food, clothing and more.

Did I turn God's bus into a book store?
God's bus, my venue of prayer, poetry, inspiration.
Did I defile God's bus by trying to sell Jesus books?

So, what should today's Church do?
Should we stop advertising bestsellers at the pulpit?
Should we stop running church like a business?

Should I stop telling people about my Jesus books?
Should I share my faith alone, I can't sell Jesus, right?
Should I give up my dream to be the poet of positive thinking?

Well, I am going to keep trying,
I am going to continue telling people of the hope.
No need to sell Jesus, salvation is for free.

CHARLIE BROWN (11)

Message: What is happiness? Today I went to Wilson High School's theatrical presentation, Charlie Brown. It was an awesome display of talent by many of my former students. Charlie Brown performed a soliloquy where he discussed the meaning of happiness. He concluded that anything and everything can be happiness, even having a pencil, that simple.

CHARLIE BROWN (11)

Happiness is being alive,
Happiness is having a lucky pen,
To write my thoughts, to inspire people.

Happiness is standing in the cold,
At 10pm waiting for a Lyft,
After an encounter with my awesome students.

Happiness is being picked up,
By a warm Lyft on route to,
Union Station to catch the Gold Line.

Happiness is boarding the Gold Line,
Riding with a man reeking of pot,
Pushing words from my scribe.

Happiness is the hope,
That I will arrive home safely and sound,
Knowing that God had my back one more day.

Happiness is watching my students perform.
Having hope that they will follow their dream,
Happiness is being alive! ☺

CHURCH ON A HARLEY (12)

Message: This poem is weird, then aren't they all? I was looking at my GPS and decided I would walk 15 minutes to another bus stop. As it often happens, the bus I was waiting for passes me up. This time I decided I would chase it down, and I won. I am glad I did otherwise I would not have met this tough bus driver.

CHURCH ON A HARLEY (12)

I saw the 187 pass me up,
I thought for a minute,
The bus would stop on the red light,
So, I revved up my engines and this old man,
Caught his limo just by its tail.

Catching my breath, "You just added years,
Of healthy living to this old man,"
"How old are you, 45? I saw you running,
Didn't think you would catch me."
She couldn't believe I was 62.

"I am tough too, God gave me a Harley.
And I go out with my friends on weekends,
To praise God on winding mountain roads,"
She didn't believe in organized religion,
But she knew God was her provider.

Church on a Harley, one of a kind,
She was in her late 50's, but like me,
Her age was not holding her back.
Me chasing my dream on a bus,
And she praising the Lord on two wheels.

COOL BUS DRIVER (13)

Message: I have dedicated several poems to bus drivers. Most of them delineate the positive attributes of drivers. Only one poem, Driver 44744 in my first book, depicts the warm welcome of a driver who proceeded to scream at me.

COOL BUS DRIVER (13)

Some bus drivers are nice and others mean,
Some cordial and others rude,
Others hospitable and some indifferent.

The first bus was running late,
Concerned I would miss my transfer,
When my bus arrived, the other bus was at the corner.

Got off the bus, ran as fast as I could,
"I saw you running so I waited," he said,
This bus driver was not only caring, but cool.

He was wearing some sun shades,
With three different colors; red, yellow and orange,
The colors blended as I saw my reflection.

"Man, you are a cool bus driver,
And those are cool sun glasses."
Thank you for waiting for me.

"I try to help whenever I can,
I would expect others to do the same for me.
Saw you running so hard, I had to wait."

I am gonna get me some cool sun glasses too,
If I am gonna ride with the best of the best,
I have to look like I am seriously cool too. ☺

COUNT YOUR BLESSINGS (14)

Message: Recently I read a book named The How of Happiness by Sonja Lyubomirsky. In this book I learned that happiness is a choice. It is like a science. We can choose what we are going to be happy about. Think of all the great things that have happened to you, they are the reasons to be happy.

COUNT YOUR BLESSINGS (14)

Ok, let's keep this simple,
Be thankful for your feet, legs, fingers, hands and arms,
Be thankful for your heart, your lungs, your stomach,
For your brain without which you couldn't do anything,

Count the many years you've been alive,
How many times have you had a good meal?
Count the times you have heard, "I love you."
Ok, how many times have you said, "I love you?"

If you're a teen, find 19 reasons to be happy,
If you're old, you have blessings untold,
If you don't see that you are blessed,
Close your eyes and open your heart.

Yes, it's as easy as that, stop and think,
Stop and count all the blessings in your life,
From the simplest of things to the complex,
There are people with less who think they have it all.

So be thankful for all that you have,
All that you have accomplished,
It's ok to look at the bad times as lessons,
But it's your choice, choose to be happy. ☺

DEEPER FOUNDATION (15)

Message: I thank God that I found Faith Community Church in West Covina, California. Pastor Jim Reeve has a special gift to put God's word into practical lessons for everyday living. He compared the foundation we have in Christ with the foundation of a skyscraper: the bigger the building, the bigger and deeper the foundation.

DEEPER FOUNDATION (15)

If you want to dream big,
You have to be well planted,
If you want to be big, you need deep roots.

The Eiffel Tower has a fifty-foot foundation,
And has been standing since March 31, 1889,
How deep does your foundation need to be?
To be standing a triumphant Christian through the years?

Will your foundation in Christ keep you strong?
During the winter and fall of life?
Will you stand erect when the big one hits?
Dig deep into yourself and your God.

The Lord Jesus is the rock of my salvation,
On solid rock I stand, He is my foundation,
My life will stand strong through the tough times,
And when the good times come, I will remember.

That my foundation is deep in Christ,
And I will stand among the tallest buildings,
When bad times come, I will be standing firm.

The challenges of life will not keep me down.

DESPERATION GOSPEL (16)

Reflection: I believe that life with God is all about prosperity, a better life, hope, faith, spiritual positive thinking. Then there are those who capitalize on justice, consequences, hell fire and brimstone. I believe that if you are right with God, even death is beautiful. Paul said, "For me to live is Christ and to die is gain."

DESPERATION GOSPEL (16)

There is no hope for a better tomorrow,
Things will never get better,
Humans have a sinful nature,
They only think of doing evil.

Hell, fire and brimstone!
God will punish all sinners,
There is no hope for salvation,
God will surely destroy the earth.

Is believing in Jesus all about damnation?
Or is it salvation from destruction?
Is it that we are all sinners?
Or can we all imitate Jesus?

It is shameful how Jesus is divided,
When in the hands of the people,
Do some belong to Paul and others to Cephas?
Do you belong to Apollos or Jesus?

Is Christ divided on the cross and broken all over again?
Jesus is hope for those in desperation,
No such thing as prosperity or desperation gospel.
Only the good news that Jesus is here for you.

TU (17)

Reflection: You have to read "Dr. Yo" first (the next poem) to appreciate "Dr. Tu." After a couple of weeks, I returned to Dr. Yo for an operation on my left eye. There was a tree (large cataract) growing in my eye that required an operation in the retina, so I was referred to a specialist, Dr. Tu. "Tú" is Spanish for "you" and "yo" means "I". You can't plan this, so these following poems were destined to tell the story of the miracle of God.

DR. TU (17)

Lord, Tú know me inside and out,
Tú formed my eyes, nose, mouth and all,
Tú planted a tree in my left retina,
Its root digging deep, ready to bear fruit.

Its fruit is words rearranged,
To say something more than just Dr. Tu,
Tú are a miracle worker, no mistake about it,
Only Tú could make a team out of Dr. Tu and Dr. Yo.

The third operation was successful too,
I can see the San Gabriel mountains,
I see the trees and telephone lines on the ridge,
I can see the wrinkles on my face and neighbors.

So, if you have cataracts don't be afraid,
Go under the knife guided by the hand of God,
I recommend Dr. Yo and Dr. Tu at Kaiser,
Who are used by Jesus to heal the blind.

"If you believe in me, greater things than these,
Will you do for the good of the world,"
Can you see clearly now? Then act!
Tell people of the mighty works of God.

DR. YO (18)

Reflection: The things that just happen by themselves are the best. I didn't plan to be born with cataracts in both eyes. And I didn't plan to be born Hispanic and be assigned a doctor named Dr. Yo. Throughout this poem I will use the Spanish word "Yo" to replace the English word "I".

DR. YO (18)

Yo brought you to this earth,
Yo knew you before you were born,
Yo knew that you would be born with cataracts,
Yo advanced medicine just for you.

Yo provided you with a doctor named Yo.
Yo guided his hand as he dug in,
Yo took a hammer to your hard head,
Yo woke you up to a miracle.

Yo knocked your friend Paul off his horse,
As he pompously rode to kill Christians,
It was Yo who took his sight away,
And returned his sight after he relinquished his pride.

Yo can heal cataracts, cancer, diabetes, hepatitis,
Lupus, malaria, colds, flus, in-grown toe nails,
Yo can heal all diseases. Yo gave humans,
The intelligence to go beyond their own wildest dreams.

"Wanna hear the truth? You were asleep.
Yo told Dr. Yo to take you to the river,
Make a ball of mud, put it on your eyes,
He washed out the mud and poof! 20/20 vision. ☺

EMPTY GRAVE (19)

Message: This Easter 2018, my son was invited to play his violin at Crossroads Community Church in Camarillo, California. The title of the pastor's sermon was "Empty". Before the pastor started his message, I was already imagining an empty grave. I was reminded that the empty grave was the one thing that makes Jesus stand out. Jesus is the only God/man who claimed to have died to save all people from their sins.

EMPTY GRAVE (19)

Did you feel empty after the loss of your wife?
Did you feel empty in school, as the bullies made sport of you?
Did you feel empty when the economy drained your pockets?
Did you feel empty because no one showed for Bible study?

Well guess what? The grave is empty too!
Jesus is no longer there! He is risen!
He is now in his Father's house preparing a place for you.
And His Holy Spirit is looking for a place to lodge.

Let Jesus come in to fill the empty absent person spot,
Let your heart be filled with the fighting love of God,
Let your life overflow with something more than money,
Let the Lord fill you with poetic words on a solitary table.

The grave is empty, death as we know it is gone!
Time to dream of another wife, new and improved,
Fear is gone, life will no longer bully you,
Now you know you are worth more than money.

So, you are not alone when you have Jesus.
If you have faith and you believe,
You can turn death into life,
Feel the power of the empty grave!

ENCOURAGEMENT (20)

Message: We are living in a world with changing values, some may say that we are losing our values. Today we live in a world of critics, everyone has an opinion. While constructive criticism may be appreciated, we need a lot more encouragers. This poem is dedicated to all my friends who have encouraged me especially my German friend Judith Neuner and Chelle Angellini from Los Angeles who posted an appreciative note on Facebook, and Don King Fisher Campbell for being my mentor. Thank you to all who have encouraged me. This one is unique because it comes clear across the Atlantic Ocean.

ENCOURAGEMENT (20)

You could have done so much better,
You have so much potential, you know?
Creative criticism, sounds good, doesn't it?
How about? "You did a great job!"
I'm proud of you, you've improved so much!

I believe people need to hear the good,
Before you give unwarranted advice,
We live in a world of criticism,
We are quick to find fault in others,
But a mirror tells the truth about us all.

Send good tithings across the Atlantic Ocean,
Encourage someone on the other side of the Pacific,
Send a little love to the hungry and the poor of the world,
Tell your neighbors how much you appreciate them,
Take a moment to put a smile on someone's face.

Thank you, Judith, for sending Germanic blessings to America,
Thank you, Don, for believing in my poetry and telling me so,
Thank you, Chelle, for advertising my Vroman's book sales,
Thank you to all my silent voices of encouragement. ☺☺☺☺

ENIGMA (21)

Reflection: I believe that Jesus is somewhat of an enigma. Is He the Son of God? If so, what does that mean? Is He a god, a prototype of divinity? Is He only the Savior? Your guess is as good as mine. Everyone, every religion claims to understand Jesus completely and they claim that they only use the Bible. Jesus is a mystery, since the time He was recorded in history, people have been trying to define the identify of Jesus. Obviously, since I have capitalized His name, adjectives and pronouns related to Him, I hold that He is the only true God.

ENIGMA (21)

Perhaps one of the most controversial,
Entities of all times and to this day,
Was He a God/man, a man/God?

Everyone who speaks of Jesus claims to be right,
Was He just the Savior or the Son of God?
What does it mean to be the Son of God?
Some claim He was a prophet, they say God has no son.

Every word Jesus enunciated seemed to clash,
His critics much larger than His entourage,
He spoke in parables, stories, analogies, allegories.

Only those who truly wanted to understand Jesus,
Didn't need explanations, logic or proof,
It is not that we don't understand Him,
We don't want to, because it requires commitment.

Perhaps Jesus is not an enigma, but we make Him so,
We argue, we bicker, we take Him apart,
We don't do that with our cars, houses, technology. ☹
It takes the simple faith of a child to understand.

FALLING (22)

Reflection: Falling is part of life but so should getting up. I have tripped and fallen so many times in life, and although I have chased the bus several times I have not yet fallen during my chase. I have fallen for pyramid schemes, fallen on the sidewalk, fallen on the stairs and even fallen in love several times. Ok, people have told me that my back stories are just like my poems and some joke and say that my first poem was better than the second. This is going to be one of those poems that will be difficult to write because I think I already wrote it.

FALLING (22)

Losing your balance because you were not paying attention,
Trying to walk straight although you had too much to drink,
Imagine how you fell when you were learning to walk,
Have you ever fallen and couldn't get up without help?

If you fall, you gotta get up no matter what,
If you broke a leg you have to walk with crutches,
But you must get up and walk any way possible,
Nick Vujicic can walk even without legs.

Did you fall for it when he said? "Prove it if you love me."
Did you fall for the lies, all those promises made?
Did you fall for that bad business deal?
Well, keep trying till you fall for the truth.

Do not let your pride hold you back,
Remember you can have God on your side,
All you have to do is ask Him for help,
Do not fall from grace like the white man with red horns.

FILLER POEM (23)

Reflection: Whenever I write poetry I struggle with indecision. Should I write this poem, is it a good one? Even when it is time to read, I can't decide which one to share, so I write everything and I publish everything. It's like my poems don't only fill the page, but also something inside me.

FILLER POEM (23)

Sometimes I write poems,
On the spur of the moment, like this one,
I am not sure I like it, it is not my best,
But my pen keeps moving, and it won't stop.

Surprise! Some people love,
Those seemingly insignificant poems,
So intentionally, I am writing one.
An empty page yearning to be filled.

Sometimes we do things, and we don't know why,
Maybe we are helping, inspiring someone,
Perhaps there is an empty spot in you,
Let my magic pen replenish your soul.

I don't want to be completely filled,
I want an empty spot somewhere in my heart,
To let a homeless man in, a person in need,
To let just a little more love in my soul.

Lord, I want to keep an empty place,
My heart open, yearning for your love,
A love I can pass on to the next guy,
To keep the momentum going.

FULL CIRCLE (24)

Moral: Ok, this is a weird poem. I am not sure what I wrote, but that is the beauty of it all. Everyone seems to have their own opinion of creation and they will swear by the Bible or whatever source is available. This poem is as confusing as all those philosophies and theories out there that claim to have all the answers. I believe in God and science but I like suspense, it keeps me on my toes.

FULL CIRCLE (24)

Where does time begin?
Where did the circle start?
What was it like in the beginning?

Does the big bang thrust through?
Changing as it flows? Transcending?
As it moves around the cosmos?

Do we just push our babies out?
Do they emerge from pre-existence?
Then we move aside to make room for more.

Was he born to wonder?
Did he live to die?
Did he resurrect to exist?

I want to live before I am born,
I want to live and die again,
And resurrect to thrive again.

Just like Jesus, the beginning and the end all over again.
I want to transcend time, to live in the world beyond,
Where there is no pain, no tears, no need for strife.

GARBAGE SYMPHONY (25)

Moral: Where there is a will there is a way. We have heard this saying several times before and Fabio Chavez a music director brings this concept to life. Cateura, a landfill in the outskirts of Asuncion, Paraguay has become the venue for music director Favio Chavez and a creative landfill carpenter, Nicolas Gomez known as "Cola", who creates dreams out of garbage. Today hundreds of disadvantaged children are now learning to play classical music using instruments made out of garbage and traveling the world entertaining kings and queens all because they lived out their dream.

GARBAGE SYMPHONY (25)

I have always had great respect for garbage,
Since my childhood, garbage was my toy.
I made slingshots out of innertubes,
Trains out of milk cartons,
Smashed bottle tops for wheels.

Today there are still people playing with garbage,
Alternative fuel made form garbage,
Plastic bottle flower pots and bird feeders,
Dwellings, chandeliers, furniture, art work,
With imagination you can make anything,

Finally, you can make music out of garbage,
A landfill named Cateura in Paraguay,
A flute made from a water tube, coins, locks, and cutlery,
A violin put together from cans, wooden spoons and forks,
Cellos out of oil drums, saxophone from drain pipe,

There is no stopping a director with a vision,
You can't stifle the creativity of a garbage carpenter,
Now poor children are playing Bach and Beethoven,
Their collective dream taking them to far-off countries,
If there is garbage in your life, imagine, just imagine…

GOD'S BAND-AID (26)

Message: In Riding the Bus 2, I published a poem about my brother Manuel. At the time I had lost contact with him due to his being deported to Mexico. I imagined a large band-aid that would cover and heal my brother's ailments, alcohol abuse and homelessness. Recently I have reunited with my brother and I see how God is gradually building that band-aid that will heal my brother permanently.

GOD'S BAND-AID (26)

Oh, if only there were a great big-o band-aid,
To heal the ailments of the world,
Or how about a band-aid big enough,
To cover my brother, his scars, addiction.

Gradually the super natural band-aid is forming,
A supportive Godly family in Tijuana,
To give my brother the love he so desires,
To give him the hope he never had.

The band-aid is being built with a little help,
God is using me to pay a little room,
To protect my brother from the dangers of the night,
He has a toilet, shower, things we take for granted.

God also needs a little help from him too,
He is the glue that holds the band-aid in place,
His determination to follow Jesus, at all costs,
Your prayers are the antiseptic pad that lies,
Right on the infected area of his heart.

Thank you to all Christian brothers and sisters,
To all my Facebook buddies who have labored with me,
Thank you, Lord, for listening to our plea.

GRANDPA IN A BOX (27)

Message: According to the World Christian Encyclopedia in 2001 there were at least 34,000 denominations of Christianity in the world. All of them claim that they believe only what the Bible says. They fail to understand that the Bible says different things to different people because the same text can be interpreted in different ways. When they disagree, they accuse each other of taking a verse out of context. I move that the greatest theologian ever lived was my three-year-old son.

GRANDPA IN A BOX (27)

We were at my father's funeral,
A solemn time, a place to be serious,
We all took turns, putting in our two cents,
The priest with his eloquent eulogy.

"Julio de Jesus Villalobos is now in a better place",
Some in the audience thinking, how do you know that?
Jehovah's Witnesses would say he is asleep,
Catholics wondering if he is in purgatory.

Atheists reassuring themselves in their beliefs,
Seventh Day Adventists asking, did he keep the Sabbath?
The Pentecostals never heard him speak in tongues,
Was he baptized in the name of Jesus or three names?

We walked up to view my father,
An elegant man in his 48X28X23 cubical,
Then the great theologian speaks out,
"Dad, did heaven put grandpa in a box?"

I know it was a painful moment, but I had to laugh,
His question left me speechless,
Everyone's theories were trampled on the floor.
So now what, the First Church of the Cuboid?

HARD TIMES POETRY (28)

Moral: It is easy to talk about the good times in our lives. The bad times we keep private, but we should share those as well. We should find a trusted friend, a clergy person or a counselor. It is not good to keep those bad feelings in. Now that I am retired I have been more open about those things that have been eating me inside.

HARD TIMES POETRY (28)

Write poetry, tell a friend, tell someone,
Let your tears drain your heart from sorrow,
Tell God in your prayers, He knows about suffering,
He suffered for our sins, he bled on the cross.

If you can remember the bad times,
Remember the good times also,
Recollect the first day of that beautiful encounter,
Talk about how God brought you out of it all.

Also, look at the good side of the bad times,
It is during those hard times that we grow,
And when we grow, sometimes we have to prune,
Cut down those branches that serve no purpose.

It is easy to tell you that my son is an awesome violinist,
But I don't want to tell you that he was suicidal,
My daughter went to the Parson's the New School,
But I am not happy that she dropped out.

My wife and I raised two children,
Don't want to talk about the divorce,
I have published three books,
But I am not the renowned writer I want to be.
Now get ready, here come the good times. ☺

HONEST PRAYER (29)

Message: When we talk to God we are praying. We need to ask the Holy Spirit to intercede for us, to teach us how to pray, to put words in our mouth. We need to glorify the name of the Lord and thank Him for what we have before we start asking for more. In the Bible there is a story about a rich man who had so much that he decided to build more shelters to store all his belongings. Little did he know that the next day he would meet his fate. Therefore, be honest, and just say what is in your heart.

HONEST PRAYER (29)

Lord God Almighty, thank you for being my only worship.
Thank you for all that You have given me to date.
Thank you for my friend, my Pastor, my confident,
That I have known since I was 19, looking at the horizon.

We are now in our 60's, at the crossroads again.
Do we invest, do we go to another country, do we trust again?
Where has our life taken us, where will we go?
Be thankful for what you have this very moment.

Thank you for this delicious breakfast here before me,
For this patio at the Corner Bakery in Glendora,
For the cars, trucks and busses passing by,
For the birds singing, and the voices of others and their stories.

We are like lilies in the fields dressed in glamour,
Like the humming birds that never stop eating,
Our Father loves us more than words,
Our wardrobe is the best, dressed in God's grace.

We don't need a great big storage place,
For things we will not own tomorrow, thank you Lord.
Thank you Lord for all that You've given me,
A treasure of blessings to take to Your Glory.
Thank you for my friend, pastor and confident.

I AM WELL-PLEASED (30)

Message: Today I heard a message regarding God's love. Right after Jesus got baptized a voice was heard from heaven, "This is my son in whom I am greatly please." Which son does not want to hear these words from his father, and which father does not want to say these words about his son? I hope my father was pleased with me over all. I was not a perfect son but I did my best. Now I am a father and I can honestly say that I am proud of my children.

I AM WELL-PLEASED (30)

My son was a three-time spelling bee winner,
His project displayed at the science fair,
Concert master with his flaming violin,
Exemplary Webelo scout, purple belt in karate,
Accepted to Los Angeles County School for the Arts.

This is my daughter, in whom I am well pleased,
Top 50 of her class, graduated with honors,
Won numerous art contests, her work on display,
Attended America's most prestigious school for fashion,
Now a full-pledged social justice activist.

If my father was alive he would be proud of me,
Author of books, father of children, teacher,
A husband, tour leader for teens, musician,
College graduate, trilingual, martial artist,
I would love to be the son in whose father is well-pleased.

This is My Son in whom I am well-pleased,
Born of the virgin Mary, growing in favor and stature,
Healer of diseases and expeller of demons,
Savior, died for the sins of the world, resurrected,
I hope my Heavenly Father will be well-pleased in me.

I BELONG (31)

Reflection: I said it once but it is worth saying again, this book is transparent. There is no need to hide any longer that I was abused emotionally, physically and sexually from the time I opened my eyes till the age of 12. I am saving the gory details for my tenth book, "Riding a Lamborghini." For a long time I dreaded being in a small or large group and having the person next to me speak. I felt insecure having all eyes staring in my direction. Now that I am retired I have set out to get total healing.

I BELONG (31)

I finally belong! To a church, a poetry club,
I am shining now, but don't let the light blind you.
Glace at me if you like and see my smile.

I belong to a poetry club,
Where it is ok to be different.
Where I can freely express my thoughts.

I belong to a church where I was allowed,
To tell my sad story of emotional, physical and sexual abuse.
Where I let it all go to set myself free.

The road lies ahead, to follow my dream,
My dream to become totally healed, to reach heights,
To help those who are looking for a place to belong.

We all belong somewhere, we just don't know it,
The cares of life have isolated us from our neighbor,
It's time to say good-bye to insecurity, poor self-image.
Say good-bye to hate, prejudice, fear, false pride.

The time has come to be humble and begin your healing. ☺

I NEED YOU (32)

Message: I am writing this backstory months after having
written this poem. By its contents I know I wrote this poem
early in the development of my fourth book. My trip to France
happened in April and now in June, I have decided to stop
procrastinating and to finish and publish my book. I realize
people can experience successful projects and trips by their own
efforts, but I acknowledge God for my success. In this poem I
admit that I need God to do everything I do.

I NEED YOU (32)

I need you Lord to lounge on this chair,
I need you Lord, to look at passersby,
I need you Lord, thank you for my legs,
As a man on a wheelchair rolls on by.

I need you Lord, to be an awesome retiree,
I need you Lord, to plan my trip to France,
I need you Lord, to finish my fourth book,
A book I hope will make your Name known.

I need you Lord, to heal my sore knee,
I need you Lord, to heal my arthritic fingers,
I need you lord, to heal my sinuses,
The way you restored my vision to 20/20.

I need you Lord, to help me be a better hubby,
I need you Lord, to help me be an exemplary father,
I need you Lord, to help me be a writer for You,
Although sometimes I feel inadequate, incapable.

I need you Lord, for everything and anything,
I need you Lord, to take my next breath,
I need you Lord, to take my next step,
Toward my destiny, to take my final breath.

I'LL SEE YOU AGAIN (33)

Message: At Faith Community Church Pastor Jim Reeve tells his church members that when they put their offering in the offering plate they should say, "I'll see you again." Although the Bible says we should not tempt the Lord it does give us permission to test God. Malachi 3:10 says that God will multiply your assets and Malachi 3:11 says He will protect your assets. Even in the secular world we say, "You get out of it what you put into it."

I'LL SEE YOU AGAIN (33)

Give God His ten percent and save another ten percent,
Take care of your church and live on eighty percent,
Give more to get more, what goes around comes around.

Give to those in need and God will give you more,
So much more, enough to give it all away,
Test God in this and He will open the floodgates of heaven.

God promises to protect your assets from corruption,
He will keep the money sharks away from your profits,
Your investments will not fail, they will flourish.

You might say, why do churches ask for money,
If "money" is the root of all evil? Wrong, you misquoted,
The "love of money" is the root of all evil.

Do you love money so much that you won't give it away?
Are all beggars on the streets really scammers?
Or do you just want to keep your money?

Maybe it is just karma, either way, I'm gonna try it!
If I am going to accomplish my dream to help the homeless,
I am going to trust God to open the floodgates of His love.

I AM A RICH MAN (34)

Reflection: Many times, I have been on the bus all by myself. This time it is special. I am on the 187 on route to Vroman's Book Store in Pasadena. I am going to commit to selling my books by consignment at Vroman's. I will have to pay a 35-dollar enrollment fee and give Vroman's 40 percent of my proceeds, in hopes that my books will be distributed throughout southern California.

I AM A RICH MAN (34)

I am a rich man!
My limo 187 is empty, all to myself,
But my driver will pick up my friends along the way,
As they wait patiently on the curb.

I'm a rich man! All for 75 cents, senior fair, ☺
All Metro/Foothill trains and buses in Southern Cal are mine!
Finally, I have reached the golden age for bus riders,
Riding a comfortable Foothill bus dirt cheap.

The public needs to be educated,
About the beauty of riding in style,
No driving insurance, no collision, no comp,
Day dreaming, napping, writing this poem.

You don't believe me?
Try it one day, take a leisure trip,
Go to the movies, to breakfast, lunch or dinner,
Go to Vroman's to purchase three crisp books.

Do not let my books collect dust on the shelf,
I want to help you, inspire you and pick you up!
And you should help me accomplish my dream,
Contribute to my Lamborghini/Tesla fund. ☺

I'M PERFECT (35)

Reflection: One of the great books of wisdom in the Bible is the book of Ecclesiastes. Chapter 7, verse 20 says, "Indeed, there is not a righteous man on earth who continually does good and who never sins." If you accept that you are not perfect, then it will be easier to accept that you are a sinner. Jesus is like a mirror that encourages you when you are doing the right things and lovingly shows you where you can improve. It is a given that I am not perfect so I need someone stronger than me in my life.

I'M PERFECT (35)

Nobody is perfect they say,
But I can prove that statement false.
I am perfect and this is why.

I am a perfect example of someone imperfect.
I can take a good thing and mess it all up.
I can preach one thing and practice another.

I am the perfect hypocrite,
I say I am going to do something,
And I do just the opposite.

I have to keep reminding myself,
That I am a flawless example if imperfection,
Often I have to go back, fix it and change it.

But there is hope, there's always hope!
As long as I accept that I am not perfect,
I can always go back to my perfect creator.

If we admit that we are not perfect,
Then God can make us clean again,
His blood is stronger than the Power of Tide®.

IF YOU'RE STILL A MAN (36)

Message: Relationships are complicated. Love is complicated. When one of the parties does not get his or her way, one of them may show their evil side. It is difficult to walk away from a broken relationship unscathed. It's important to say good-bye in style without holding grudges. Let go of the past and move forward, it is the only way to go if you want healing and a new start.

IF YOU'RE STILL A MAN (36)

Love is so beautiful and fresh,
The first stare in the eyes, first kiss.
Holding hands, walking in the breeze,
Wind sifting through one's hair.

Promises made, marriage plans ahead,
Exchanging gifts, meeting friends and family,
Going on dates, traveling to exotic places,
Can't see the future, but willing to take risks.

Suddenly without warning, red flags,
Dancing in the wind, at first ignored,
Little insignificant things climbing,
To the mountain peaks, glancing at the horror.

Time to reevaluate yourself, is this the one?
Slow down, take a step back, take a break,
If this is the right one, love and trust will endure,
Trust, and God will show you the way.

Then the insults begin, "If you're still a man…."
Distrust steps in, you have to regain the trust,
Anger rises, finally the breakup, then…?
Good-bye, nice knowing you, wish you the best. ☹

INSOMNIA (37)

Message: Ever since I can remember, I have never had enough sleep. Since I retired though, I have been sleeping like never before. Since the time I was a child, working in the cold and hot fields, to college, as a teacher, I have sacrificed my sleep. I have lost needed sleep all of my life, until now!☺

INSOMNIA (37)

Turning over in your bed,
Counting sheep, monitoring the clock,
Watching TV, reading a book, playing FreeCell,
Nothing seems to work, eyes wide open.

Did I eat too much, drink too much?
The Sominex pills are not working,
Maybe I should take a warm shower,
A warm glass of milk with cookies?

I began to think, this is a good time to pray,
Quiet night, I can think, perhaps write,
I can watch YouTube videos on motivation,
Maybe videos on how to fall asleep.

Insomnia, hmm? in-some-knee-a,
In-some-knee-a man is crying out to God,
In-some-knee-a woman is at the feet of Jesus,
In-some-knee-a broken heart is pleading.

You see, you are not sleep deprived, you are in prayer,
Take this time to thank God for your life,
Tell God about your loved ones,
Tell God how much you love Him.

In-some-knee-a people is seeking God.

JAZZ (38)

Message: This poem was originally written at a workshop held at Santa Catalina Branch Library, sponsored by Don Kingfisher Campbell. The original poem was misplaced, hopefully not permanently. Last I remember, I was sharing it with the Bible Club at Woodrow Wilson High School. The writing prompt was a jazz concert being held at the Pasadena Branch Library. Since I am now writing "Riding the Bus with Jesus", here is my attempt to "Jesusize" this jazz concert.

JAZZ (38)

As I sat there pondering,
It hit me hard on the head like a rock!
Jazz: Jesus and zebras. Stripes!

How do zebras get their stripes?
Do they enter the gene pool?
Are their stripes camouflage for protection?

Not Jesus, He earned His 50 stripes
Through a centurion, determined to make Jesus pay.
If you believe it, he suffered for your sins.

Zebras usually run in packs,
When the enemy strikes, they all run.
Only one or two become dinner.

Not Jesus, He suffered alone,
His disciples did not run with him,
There was no chance for escape.

Therefore, if you believe in Jesus and zebras,
Appreciate the value of their stripes,
Empathize with Jesus on route to His final jazz.

JESUS WAS A POET (39)

Message: Jesus was not easy to understand, because he spoke in parables, and often spoke in the third person when referring to Himself. He used symbolism to portray messages and only those who wanted to understand could interpret his words properly. Jesus will be remembered for His words that defended the underdog and condemned the oppressor. Jesus was a rebel and if He were physically on earth today He would not conform to the present world system.

JESUS WAS A POET (39)

"The Son of Man is the Lord of the Sabbath,
How much more valuable is a person than a sheep?
Whoever is not with me is against me,
Blasphemy of the Holy Spirit will not be forgiven,"
To this day the words of Jesus have to be interpreted,
And to this day, people do not agree on their meaning.

If Jesus was going to heal somebody, he did it in style,
"Stretch out your hand," to heal a withered hand,
"Go your way, as you believed, so it will be done for you,"
"Take up your mat and walk," to a lame man,
"Go wash in the pool of Siloam," to the blind man,
Jesus did not refer his patients to a specialist.

If you are a poet or someone who needs inspiration,
Go to the Man who walked on water,
To the Man who fed thousands with a few fish,
Who could pick out a hypocrite in a crowd,
If you are in the middle of a storm,
I know a Man who can calm the sea.

Let Him calm the storms in your life.

JESUS TODAY (40)

Reflection: On mount Calvary, the day Jesus was crucified two thieves were also crucified with him, one on His right hand the other on His left. One of them mocked Jesus while the other defended Him and asked for His mercy. Jesus promised him that he would be in paradise. If you know this passage well, you might have noticed that people might argue whether the comma should go before or after the word "today".

JESUS TODAY (40)

"I assure you, today you
shall be with me in paradise."
"I assure you today,
you shall be with me in paradise."

Whatever the case, if Jesus promises,
Your today will come today,
In one year, ten years, in heaven,
Rest assured, it is coming.

So, whatever you need,
Ask and it shall be given,
Believe and it will happen,
Not your way, but His.

Today Jesus can come to save your soul,
Today Jesus can make a difference in your life,
It doesn't matter where you put the comma,
Today, He knows what's best for you. ☺

You can trust in Jesus today!

LADY IRON (41)

Message: In the year I retired (graduated from teaching ☺) I accomplished one of my dreams to take my family on a tour to France. I wanted them to see why I loved France so much. My son had already gone with me on one of my student tours and it was an easy task to convince my wife and daughter that France was an awesome country. One of the main attractions was the Eiffel Tower of course, over 500 dollars for dinner, top floor, first night. In this poem I will attempt to demonstrate the majesty of such a structure and how it can be applied to everyday living.

LADY IRON (41)

Construction began on the 28th of January, 1887,
Digging fifty feet for its foundation,
Surveying the land underneath for faults,
Two years, two months, five days later,
Finished on the 31st of March, 1889,
First technical feat of its kind,
1710 steps and 18,000 pieces of iron held together,
Standing at 984 feet, 1,063 to the tip of her antenna,
The tallest building in the world for 41years,
Celebrating 100 years after the French Revolution,
Main attraction of the Paris Exposition, World Fair,
7,300 tons of wrought iron, total weight 10,100 tons,
Every seven years 60 tons of paint,
More than 7 million people visit Lady Iron every year,
Passing 250 million since its opening in 1889,
Over 2,500,000 bolts, nuts and rivets hold it together.

So, if you want to stand tall it is going to take some effort,
How many bolts and nuts will it take to keep you together?
How many years do you need to become your dream?
How deep is your foundation, your values and convictions?
Reach out! And touch God in the skies! ☺

LAZARUS (42)

Reflection: Most people know the story of Lazarus who had been dead for four days. Jesus asked the mourners to roll away the stone and He shouted, "Lazarus, come out!" Immediately Lazarus came out of the tomb as if he had never died. A friend of mine in college had an old car that he named Lazarus. Often his clunker would shut off at a stop sign, he would get off, open the trunk and pray, "Lazarus, wake up!" and it would fire up !☺

LAZARUS (42)

Those college years were tough.
Where would our meals come from?
How would we make ends meet?
Would we walk, ride, bus it or drive?

He was like most of us,
But he decided he wanted to drive.
Got the oldest beat up car he could find,
A cartoon character who chugged and tugged along.

In the Bible there are stories of Jesus,
Bringing people back to life like new.
Jesus' dear friend Lazarus,
The daughter of the centurion.

What do you need from God?
To bring to life your lost dreams?
Do you want your relationship renewed?
Do you want your stove and fridge to last longer?

By faith my friend would take,
His clunker on the road to chug along.
It earned its name, "Lazarus, wake up!"
And Lazarus would come back to life like new! ☺

LI'L JOB 1 (43)

Reflection: Do you know anyone who has struggled through life seemingly doing all the right things? The book of Job in the Bible tells such a story. I believe there have been several prototypes of Jobs that I call "Li'l Jobs". When things go sour even when we are doing our best, I like to imagine that the devil and God are having a debate about the faithfulness of one of us. In the end the good guy always wins.

LI'L JOB 1 (43)

He did what was right,
He behaved well in school,
Finally enrolled in college,
Wasn't easy but he kept moving forward.

All of a sudden, the economy fell,
He wasn't ready, no emergency savings,
His son became depressed, suicidal,
His daughter dropped out of college.

Finally, his wife left him,
All those years of sublime investments,
His dream to have a perfect family,
Gone! With the troubles of life.

God turns to the devil and says,
"See my faithful servant?
He hasn't turned his back on me."
He shares his sad story with others,
Then he concludes, "I am trusting in Jesus."

If you are going through a hard time,
Hold true to your dreams and values.
Imagine God debating about you with the enemy.

LI'L JOB 2 (44)

Moral: The first "Li'l Job" was already written and misplaced, but now this new poem is taking a different tone. With my son's depression, and the divorce behind me, "Li'l Job 2" becomes an answered prayer. It is important to note though, that the past needs to be placed in the past, otherwise it will go with you into the present and the future. If you are going through depression or a divorce at this moment, keep in mind that this too will pass; time will win for you.

LI'L JOB 2 (44)

One day the devil came to God.
"Watchupta ol' chum?"
"I'm going around to see who I can trip up,"
"Have you noticed my servant Luis?
He's just trying to do his best."

"Yeah, but you've given him everything!"
"Ok, give his whole family depression,
Separate him from his wife, his love,
You'll see that he won't turn his back on Me."
So, the devil set out to mess! him! up!

Life started to happen to Luis,
His college degree could not comfort his soul,
His job, money, house, students not enough,
He felt God had turned his eyes on someone else.

Time passed and Luis got closer to God,
Things have leveled off, hope in sight,
Children doing good, wife peaceful, faith increased,
The devil got angry, and said, "The heck with this guy!"
Quickly he went to ask for permission to go to the next guy.

Stay faithful to your faith and you will win!☺

LI'L JOB 3 (45)

Message: After having misplaced my first "Li'l Job" poem, I wrote my second one not knowing that I would find the first one again. Like a miracle the second one fits perfectly with the first. It is like the stages of Job in the Bible. Now I am thinking that there has to be a third one that is somewhat prophetic. The first one I wrote right after the divorce which was quite devastating. The second poem was written after my healing from depression. Now, the third one imagines what an ideal life will look like. Let's see what happens in the years to come.

LI'L JOB 3 (45)

The divorce knocked him to his knees,
Recovery helped him conquer fear, to take risks,
Now only the future is at hand.

Will he accomplish his dream, to remarry his wife?
Will his son and daughter finish their careers?
Will he make millions flipping real estate?

Not once did Job turn his back on God,
And he prayed for those who were accusing him,
Then the Lord gave him twice as much as he had before.

After the Lord restored Job, he lived 140 years more,
Job's friends, brothers and sisters came and brought,
Gold and silver and celebrated his recovery.

Will Luis someday throw a big party,
Invite his friends, brothers and sisters?
Will he live to be 100 and see his grandchildren too?
Will he stand next to his beloved wife?
Will he become the "givenaire" he dreamed about?
We will see. Come on Lord, do Your stuff! ☺

LOOK AT ME (46)

Moral: Poetry is a place where one can grow and be honest. A miracle happened when I came to saturdayafternoonpoetry.com. This is the first place where I felt totally comfortable with myself and others. Poetry is a heaven where you can become yourself.

LOOK AT ME (46)

Look at me if you want to,
If you want to judge me or not,
We are all people wearing,
Hats of hair and other coverings.

A cloud of ideas lie beneath our hats,
You can be yourself, I can be myself,
You can act like Mickey Mouse if you want,
Look at me because I feel your love.

Look at me, I am transparent,
Now, I know it's not about me,
It's about us listening to each other,
We all have so much to share!

Look at each other, have compassion,
Don't be afraid to talk and share,
No need to feel nervous or insecure,
This is where I can look at you,

And you are free to look at me,
I will not feel insecure if you look in my direction,
My face will not turn red and my eyes blue,
Can you also feel the way Jesus looks at me?

LOSING (47)

Message: This is not about losing. It's about gaining, but in life sometimes we lose things, opportunities, and loved ones. This week I lost a student. There has been talk that the French program will be lost next year. To stay on top of things I need to remember all that God has given me. What I lose is not as important as the blessings I receive.

LOSING (47)

In life we lose things,
A loved one, a job, opportunities,
We lose patience, hope, vision.

Depression sets in,
Can't see the solution,
To a problem that gets worse.

She fought cancer to the end,
Chemotherapy, bone marrow transfer,
Recovered, finally lost the battle.

But did she really?
She is in a better place now,
A place of rest and no pain.

When in pain remember the Corinthians,
Faith, hope and the greatest of these is love,
Losing is life but God is love,

Never lose the hope of God's love.

LUCKY OR NOT (48)

Message: This is another poem that was written at a writing workshop in Santa Catalina Branch Library. It was written for the purpose of being published in the ensuing edition of Spectrum Publishing. The title of the edition was Lucky or Not so I decided to write a poem named by the title and it made it to publication. I imagined that the final destiny of every living person was to die and to appear before an All Mighty God. I want to look good when my turn comes.

LUCKY OR NOT (48)

Whether you are lucky or not,
Whether you are rich or poor,
Whether you win or lose.

Whether you are tall or short,
Whether you are healthy or sick,
Whether you are hopeful or hopeless.

The world will keep turning,
The rich become poor and the poor rich,
When you win you lose, when you lose you win.

You start out life tall and strong,
Then you lose cartilage, get arthritis,
And the wiles of life will make you short again.

Whether you are this or that,
One thing is for sure, "You gonna die!"
So therefore, give your soul to Jesus,

You can't get luckier than that.
Your future is in His hands,
Salvation is at hand.☺

MADRE (49)

Message: This is the only poem in Spanish that will appear in Riding the Bus with Jesus. I dedicated it to all mothers and all they could possibly be. And I pay homage to my own mother who gave me the advice to never argue with my wife if I wanted to be happy, because I was always going to lose.

MADRE (49)

Mujer virtuosa, ¿Quién la encontrará?
Bendita entre todas las mujeres,
Con sus manos edifica su hogar,
El corazón de su esposo en ella confía.

Sus hijos como retoños al derredor de su mesa,
Con su voz alienta a sus hijos,
Su canto es dulce como los ángeles,
Mujer que obedece al Señor.

Madre que salva a su pueblo,
Mujer que encuentra gracia delante de Dios,
Madre escritora, profesora, filósofa,
Actriz de la vida real.

Abogada, astronauta, diplomática, activista,
Compositora, productora, empresaria, filántropa,
Directora, doctora, dentista, aviadora,
Líder, monarca, heroína, reina, física,
Matemática, química, ¿qué no puede hacer una mujer?

Pero más que nada la madre da la vida,
Sin ella no podríamos ni escribir o leer un poema,
Gracias a mi madre por su consejo, "¿Si quieres,
Ser feliz, nunca alegues con tu mujer,
Porque siempre vas a perder."☺

MOTIVATION WITH JESUS (50)

Reflection: The concept of motivation may be as old as 10 centuries but the "lack of motivation" is probably as old as the Garden of Eden. I believe that everyone struggles with a lack of motivation. This book that I am now writing should have been finished three years ago. My life's challenges have kept me from my dream to publish ten books. Well, that's enough procrastination. This horse is going to the river and it is going to get its fill of water.☺

MOTIVATION WITH JESUS (50)

"You can lead a horse to water,
But you can't make it drink."
This saying is meant for people.
Can't force anyone to do anything.

Yet, I still keep writing,
Motivating myself and others,
To go beyond their own limits,
Writing about the unreachable.

Are my students motivated?
Do my children inherently do their best?
Do my poems motivate people to change?
Do motivated people find reassurance?

You can't force a horse to drink,
But you can deny it water to make it thirsty.
Maybe people need to deny themselves,
Less of the good life, to gain more desire.

So therefore, I know it is my destiny,
To publish this book and to help people,
So, I am looking for a drink, I'm thirsty,
And I am going to satiate myself with living water. ☺

MY EVERYTHING (51)

Moral: There are times when things get so complicated that I feel I have nothing. In retrospect, that is the best place to be because that is when I realize that all I need is Jesus. He becomes my everything, he is my everything. At the end of the race everyone will be going totally alone to face God even if surrounded by people. When we are born we come with nothing and so when we die we will take nothing. But that is the beauty, because all we really need is Jesus. ☺

MY EVERYTHING (51)

Lord Jesus, you are my savior,
My deliverer, my provider, my refuge,
You are my protector, my security.

You are my food, my sustainer,
My cup of life, my sense of it all,
My reason for living, my hope.

Lord Jesus, you are my strength,
You are my encourager, my cheerer,
You applaud my accomplishments.

You are my forgiver, my eraser of sins,
My escape, my way out,
You are my opportunity, my way in.

You are many things I can't put into words,
You are my past, present and future,
You are! Did I leave anything out?

You are my everything!
You are my,
Everything!!!!

MY FEET (52)

Reflection: Some people see believing in God as a crutch. I used to say that. "I don't need crutches to walk, I can do it on my own." Later in my years when I needed direction in my life I went to God for the guidance that only He could provide. If you are looking for answers in life maybe you can give Jesus a chance. God became my feet, not my crutches.

MY FEET (52)

I've never really had it together,
Like most, I have gone through the motions,
If I was sad or depressed it was normal,
Yet deep inside I was looking for the answer.

Traumatic childhood, years of sexual abuse,
All buried in the past, like it never happened,
But life caught up with me, the insecurity,
The despair, the need for someone stronger than me.

I remembered when I said I didn't need crutches,
When I gave my life to Jesus he became my new feet,
I was right, I didn't need crutches, I needed feet,
I needed someone supernatural to oversee me.

As time went by I learned to trust,
Even though things may not be perfect,
I have a hope that things will be alright,
My Lord guides me every step of the way.

So, if you want a good set of feet,
I know someone who has walked in everybody's shoes,
In the words of long passed Christian rocker, Larry Norman,
"Why don't you look into Jesus, He has the answer."

ON THE ROAD AGAIN (53)

Reflection: The word "again" can be a good word or a bad word. It depends how such a word is used. Philippians 4:4 says, "Rejoice in the Lord always, again I say rejoice." Some people start drinking again after a period of rehabilitation. Now that my son has gotten his driver's license and inherited my Prius, I can ride the bus, again, and that is a good thing.

ON THE ROAD AGAIN (53)

I am on the road again, doing what I like,
Riding, writing, napping, dreaming,
I am sharing my stories with fellow riders.

My son is off to the horizon,
He is scaling highways and byways,
In search of his own dream, his destiny.

Sometimes in life we lose sight of our vision,
We get caught up in the monotony of life,
We get lost in the routine of survival.

But if you have a calling you will come back,
You will find your way once again,
If it was meant to be, it will be.

So, I'm back on my limo again,
Continuing the dream of being a writer,
Author of "Riding the Bus with Jesus."

Again, traveling the narrow road,
Pushing my lucky pen for Jesus,
Riding with all kinds of people, my inspiration.

ONE MORE (54)

Message: The Bible in the book of Proverbs says, "Trust in the Lord with all your heart and lean not on your own understanding, in all your ways acknowledge Him and He will make your paths straight." This is a good promise for me to keep when I am at the crossroads. Major decisions can affect our lives forever. It is important that I have someone that I can trust no matter what. Therefore, I am putting my trust in the one that knows everything.

ONE MORE (54)

One more reason to trust,
A new challenge gets in your way,
One more reason to believe.

Things can't be perfect all the time,
New trials will come along,
In conflict? Remember your triumphs.

Things will be fine, believe,
But work diligently, seek counsel,
To find the solution to your problem.

One more, one more reason to pray,
One more, one more reason to dream,
One more, one more reason to try.

Someday you'll look back,
Today will only be a memory,
Tomorrow will be a better day.

Therefore, I challenge you to trust,
In the one who can change everything,
I know He's got your back, He's got mine.

ONE TALENT (55)

Moral: Mathew 25:14 tells the parable of the talents. The word talent has evolved from an ancient weight and unit of currency to a natural aptitude or skill. If talent implies natural aptitude and skill, then there is where you should invest your time and money. The message that I got from this parable is that God wants me to use my talents wisely. One day I think He will ask me what I did with my talents.

ONE TALENT (55)

What are you doing with your talents, what will you do?
Will you look to the past, analyze your mistakes?
Will you organize your present for an awesome future?
Well, if that is your plan, there's a lot of wisdom out there.

Jesus compares success to a proprietor entrusting his assets,
To three servants who were given a certain amount of talents,
One received five talents, another, two and the last one,
What will you do with the talents God gives you?

The one who received five talents became an investor,
I want to take the five talents God gave me and double,
His investments to bless others, help the homeless,
I want God to be well-pleased in me.

If I was the second servant who received two talents,
I would not be jealous that God gave the other more,
I would faithfully work my talents and be thankful,
But if He wants to give me more, I am down with that!

Finally, don't be envious that you were entrusted with one,
If you believe in your talents you can do the same as well,
I don't want to hide the talents that You gave me Lord,
Whatever You give me Lord, I want to use it for Your Glory.

POOR BOY/FRENCH FATHER (56)

Reflection: This type of poetry is called "building block". The idea is to write a sentence depicting a major event in your life. I wrote two sentences: one about how I used to make my own toys and the other about how I would spend much of my time at my French father's house, across the street. I thank Don King Fisher Campbell for organizing saterdayafternoonpoetry.com at Santa Catalina Branch Library of Pasadena, California and I thank Karl Stilwell "Calokie" for leading the workshop today.

POOR BOY/FRENCH FATHER (56)

Poor,
Poor boy,
Poor boy climbs,
Poor boy climbs tree,
Poor boy climbs tree cuts,
Poor boy climbs tree cuts branch,
Poor boy climbs tree cuts branch for,
Poor boy climbs tree cuts branch for bow,
Poor boy climbs tree cuts branch for bow and,
Poor boy climbs tree cuts branch for bow and arrow.

Go,
Go down,
Go down stairs,
Go down stairs to,
Go down stairs to sidewalk,
Go down stairs to sidewalk to,
Go down stairs to sidewalk to cross,
Go down stairs to sidewalk to cross to,
Go down stairs to sidewalk to cross to visit,
Go down stairs to sidewalk to cross to visit French,
Go down stairs to sidewalk to cross to visit French father.

PROCRASTINATING WITH JESUS (57)

Reflection: In my first three books an underlying theme related to dreams and goals coming true is that of procrastination. The best way to make a dream come true is to work at it. Even Jesus, when He performed miracles He had people do things like putting mud on a man's eyes and asking him to go wash in the river. If we procrastinate at work we may get reprimanded. If I am going to delay dreams in my life it is as if I am procrastinating with Jesus. I must pick up my pace and keep going through His Grace.

PROCRASTINATING WITH JESUS (57)

Procrastination is a big problem,
Many people wait to the last minute.
"I'll do it tomorrow, I'm too tired.
Someone else can do it better later."

But your dreams cannot wait,
They have to get done now.
Your boss won't wait,
He wants it now.

Did you make a promise in the name of Jesus?
It is like swearing, now you have to get it done,
Better not promise if you're not sure,
The only way to do it is through God's grace.

What did you promise to do?
Are you going to finish your book now?
Are you going to flip houses like you flipped students?
Now flip your words into dreams accomplished,

Repent of your procrastination with Jesus,
Take a leap of faith, take action,
Into the new you. ☺

PROSTERITY GOSPEL (58)

Moral: It is a shame that Christians spend so much time pointing fingers at other churches. Small churches may criticize mega churches for being materialistic, and mega churches may assure that small churches lack vision. I propose what Jesus said, "If they are not against us, they are for us."

PROSTERITY GOSPEL (58)

Whatever you do will prosper,
Whatever you sow you will reap,
Whatever you declare will happen.

You will have plenty of food,
You will have a great big-o house,
You will have nice cars,
You will have money to give away.

I think sour people will disagree,
But Job got everything back and more,
And all a blind man wanted was to see,
The lame man picked up his mat and jumped for joy!

Perhaps the prosperity gospel does exist,
Maybe you can be content with just a little more,
When you get that one little thing you always wanted.
What is wrong with asking God for your dream?

Do you propose a desperation gospel?
Then what is the good news that Jesus brought to mankind?
Stop pointing fingers, it is a shame that people judge God,
By His children's works, failure to love others as themselves. ☹

RETIRE MINT TEA (59)

Reflection: I have been working hard since I was ten years old, getting up at four in the morning, in freezing temperatures to endure the hot blazing sun in the late mornings and afternoons. From the rising early to engage in farm labor to the rising early and the staying up late of the academic world, it was time to retire and sleep, enjoy life and work smart. Now it is time to flip houses for fun, it is not about the money.

RETIRE MINT TEA (59)

I always thought that I would,
Catch up with my lost sleep after death,
Those long sleepless nights in high school,
College no sleep, teaching no sleep.

Now I retire to my mint tea and sleep,
Then I wake up and go back to sleep,
Then I wake up and sleep some more,
I want a head start, have a lot of sleeping to do.

I once got involved in one of those pyramids,
The C.E.O. would brag of financial freedom,
"I get up when I am finished sleeping", he said,
I dreamed of sleeping on a cloud till I was done.

Now I am on the Gold Line on route,
To the superintendent's retirement reception,
I am feeling sleepy again, time to relax,
Yawning, the breeze feels good on my teared eyes.

I'm back! Took a 15-minute nap, then a four-minute walk,
Walked the red carpet, sitting on a red seat,
At the Ramon Cortinez School for the Performing Arts,
The MC is on the podium, "Let the party begin!" ☺

RIDING THE 907 TO CHULA VISTA (60)

Message: I thank God that I have made the choice to experience public transportation. The comfort of my personal cubical in my car would not afford me the opportunity to interact with people the way that I do on a public bus. Now I am on my way from Tijuana to Chula Vista to drop off my laptop at Best Buy. I think someone tried to hack into my computer in Tijuana while I was trying to go online.

RIDING THE 907 TO CHULA VISTA (60)

Riding the bus to Chula Vista,
Is pretty much like everywhere else,
A girl with green hair,
A young man all decked out in a suit.

White people, Black people, Hispanics,
Asians, teens, white kid on a skateboard,
Almost everyone with cell phone on hand,
Me?, with my lucky pen in my hand.

Old people, young people, conversations,
English, Spanish, profanity at the back of the bus,
Bus goes past shopping center, countryside,
Poor neighborhood, and the rich on the mountain sides.

Lord, why so much diversity, so much contrast?
Why some rich, why some poor and middle class?
Lord, I ask you once again, watch over us all,
I wish I could do something more than just write.

I want to make a difference before I leave planet earth,
I know Jesus said that the poor would be with us forever,
But that doesn't mean we don't have to do anything,
On the contrary, He wants us to be good Samaritans.

RIDING THE FAST TRAIN TO BIARRITZ (61)

Reflection: I am now retired so it is time to begin enjoying life in a totally new way. I am on my way to Biarritz now to visit two cities I fell in love with when I was 19, Biarritz and Saint-Geours-de-Maremne. I want my family to get a glimpse of my love for France and French culture. Please enjoy my reflections as I share a state-of-the-art train with pioneers like myself. I find that people are the same and different just like anywhere else.

RIDING THE FAST TRAIN TO BIARRITZ (61)

Riding the fast train to Biarritz,
What could be better than,
Riding the train with my family?

I want them to see the beauty,
Of the up and down streets by the beach,
To have them share in my dream.

The countryside of Saint-Geours-de-Maremne,
To meet the Pedeluc's, my adopted family,
To give my little brother the raft he wanted.

The arrival from Paris to Biarritz was 1600,
That's 6pm, right? No! it's 4pm!
What was I thinking? We had to rush out!

A lady chases me out the door,
"Donnez-moi mon valise!"
I ran back in to get my daughter's bag.

What a scare! The Frenchie's thought we were crazy,
I knew 1600 was 4pm, not 6mp, an awesome tour guide, I am!
My family just laughed at me, with me and forgave me. ☺

RIDING THE METRO LINK (62)

Message: Throughout my poems you will see stories highlighting different forms of transportation. You will see poems about walking, running, bicycles, motorcycles, cars, trains, boats and planes. At this moment I am on the Metrolink train. Just like the bus, I have time to think and reflect. It is during these quiet moments that I am inspired to write and grow. And yes, I am riding the Metro Link with Jesus. ☺

RIDING THE METRO LINK (62)

To me it is mindboggling,
How people move through the neighborhood,
The city, the county, the state, country and world,
Everyone going in different directions,
On foot, bicycle, motorcycle, car, bus, boat, plane,
Everyone moving and traveling for different reasons.

I am on the Metrolink on route to Starbucks,
Where my wife will pick me up.
I am praying, "Lord, my life is in your hands,
My wife's life is in your hands."
My son and daughter watching to see,
If forgiveness and restauration is at hand.

I began to wonder about others on the train,
Where are they going? One, to his niece's baseball game,
Looking through the window at the scenery,
Garbage along the wall, the Baldwin Park flee market,
Nurseries, industrial areas, schools, residential,
I remember when I took a joy ride with my 5-year-old.

The world turning and people coming and going.
Life is a series of good memories you wanna hold on to,
The bad memories, you have to let them go,
Leave them behind on the next bus, train, plane, or boat.

ROUND INFINITY (63)

Message: In Riding the Bus 3, I published a poem called Round #15. It is based on Rocky Balboa who would get beat up silly until the 15th round where he would either tie or win by a knockout. In the Christian life we fight through grace and you never lose because there is always one more round with God's help. If you get knocked out God is going to keep counting until you get up again.

ROUND INFINITY (63)

In professional boxing there are only 15 rounds,
In the end it is a tie, win by points or a knockout.
One! Two! Three! Motionless,
Four! Five! Six! Seven! Still down,
Eight! Nine! Ten! You are declared the winner!

Life is like a boxing ring.
You hit, and you get hit harder,
It is anybody's guess who will win.
The one with more breath, saliva, energy,
Has the potential to knock out the opponent.

In the Christian life, there is only one winner,
Grace will keep counting for you until you win.
Therefore, if life keeps knocking you over, "Get up!"
You are not going to lose, God's on your side,
Finances, illness, relationships cannot steal your dream.

Get up and fight! Because Jesus is counting to infinity!
If you have faith, He will give you the strength to rise,
Look back, remember all the battles you have won,
You may think you won them all on your own,
But no, Jesus was there, right in your corner.

RUNNING AGAIN AND AGAIN (64)

Message: I have so many poems with the concept of "again", in my first, second and third books. I just had to write another poem, again. In many cases we have to do something several times, it is not enough to do it once. In life we go through several tests again and again to make us better. Obviously, riding the bus is no different. Sometimes you have to run if you want to be a good bus rider.

RUNNING AGAIN AND AGAIN (64)

The 61-year-old man who looks 50,
Is running after the bus with all his might,
Caught the 187 just in seconds,
And he had to run to catch the 280.

Life is a race to the finish,
Again, I had to run back to the 280,
Running out of breath,
I asked the driver for more oxygen.

The second driver saw me,
When I got off the 187,
I waived him down and ran,
As fast as I could, first, second, third gear.

I told him he was the coolest bus driver,
He wore cool, yellow, orange and red shades,
I asked him if he could give me another transfer,
He said it was against policy, but he was still cool.

"I can afford an extra $1.25, I'm rich!
That's why I ride a limo with all my friends,
Soon I will be 62, 50 cents a ride,
And I'm going to get cool glasses just like you too." ☺

SAYING GOOD-BYE (65)

Message: This dating thing is very complicated. Thousands of books have been published on the subject. YouTube is saturated with good and bad advice. When couples end a relationship it is for the better in the long run. Rather than regretting the past, write a poem about it. ☺

SAYING GOOD-BYE (65)

Relationships start with passion,
Promises are made, all we see is stars.
The soul is filled with hope,
Pessimism is annihilated with love.

Then the tests come, the disappointments.
You are no longer compatible with your loved one.
Time reveals obstacles you didn't notice before,
It looks bleak, you don't think you can resist.

Some get lucky I guess, they come back,
The mystery there, no one understands.
Love covers all offences, the Bible says.
Love endures all, believes all, trusts all.

But we are not talking about humans here.
God is love, only God can bring you back together.
When there is no hope, there is God's love.
No one loses here, life goes on.

It's now time to say good-bye.
Maybe you can be friends in another life.
God loves you both equally.
Good thing it didn't end up in marriage.

SH$T BOOKS (66)

Moral: Thank God I am a poet with a good sense of humor. It is an art to take a bad situation and flip it into a good one. Not everyone I meet is a lover of my poetry, of course. Unfortunately, I have met three individuals who have told me so. The title of this poem is dedicated to the grand-prize winner!

SH$T BOOKS (66)

"Why do you ride the bus,
And write poetry, man? That's embarrassing!
Get a car, even an old one,
And drive to work like everyone else."

I approached excited, "Look,
I published my third book!"
"Oh, I don't have time,
To read that kind of garbage."

"And stop publishing sh$t books!"
This is the grand-prize winner!
Why do people go out of their way?
To hurt each other instead of encourage?

I am very fond of my poetry,
But sometimes I feel quite insecure.
These kinds of comments don't help me,
My poetry is the secretion of spirit, mind and soul.

Never thought of my poetry as bowel movements,
Well, maybe we do need sh$t books,
To deposit the crap and garbage,
That sometimes life can bring us.

SHANGHAINESE MARY MAGDALENE (67)

Moral: China is one of the most peaceful countries I have visited.
Nobody has guns, not even the police. I didn't see one fight. I
met up with three beggars and one prostitute. When the
prostitute approached me, I ignored her and went on my way.
This poem is about what I wish I would have done.

SHANGHAINESE MARY MAGDALENE (67)

A beautiful Mary Magdalene approached me,
And gave me a sexy look. She asked if she could join me,
Told her I was with my girl and ignored her.
Why did I say that? That was not in my heart.
I don't use woman for sex.

Instead I wish I would have said,
"I will have sex with you only for love.
You will be my girl and we will wed.
You will no longer work like this,
And you will be the mother of our children."

Or, "You are so beautiful, why do you do this?
Your sins are forgiven, go and sin no more.
Jesus loves you in a way you do not know.
He died and suffered for you on a cross.
Your life can be different from this day on."

Or, "Open your heart to Jesus, give your life to Him,
Leave the past behind, today is a new day.
Meet me at the well, I have living water.
Where are those who accuse you? I don't accuse you either".
But not the stupid thing I said. ☹☹☹☹

SHE LIKES ROSES (68)

Message: Love is such a beautiful thing, a difficult and complicated subject. There are no guarantees except that you have to work at it if you want a chance at it. Love is like a rose bush and its flowers, they have to be tended to and taken care of. If you have love, take care of it because it can easily fade away. But if it does fade you can always start again in the spring.

SHE LIKES ROSES (68)

Would that I were I rose,
So, she would nurture me,
Water me, move the soil around me,
Spray me with organic vitamin water,
To prolong my longevity and keep me strong.

Would that I were a cluster of roses,
So, she would stick her nose inside me,
Run me against her lips and cheeks,
To arouse her love for me,
Take me in her arms avoiding the drought of life.

Would that I were a dormant rose bush,
To give her hope in the winter,
To once again spring up,
To bring joy to her eyes, smile on her lips,
For her hand to touch me once again.

I would let her trim my branches,
To make my flower more beautiful,
I would be willing to give my life,
To be a perfumed ointment on her body,
Like alabaster oil for the feet of Jesus.

SPENDING ANONYMOUS (69)

Message: In my previous books I have talked about money before. Perhaps the title of this poem should be "Spending on credit anonymous". Even when we run out of money we won't stop. We were taught that we can get whatever we want now and pay later. Sometimes I think that money and credit are scams. Why do banks and credit card companies keep lending money if they know they may not get paid back?

SPENDING ANONYMOUS (69)

The new shoes in the closet you never used,
A garage full of piled-up junk,
Those Christmas gifts no one will ever use,
People spend like there is no tomorrow.

I constantly have to remind myself,
To stick to my rigid budget,
It is easy to get caught up in the rat race,
Materialism replacing things that really matter.

Along with NA and AA, there should be SA.
"Spending Anonymous" for those relentless spenders,
SA for those who are slaves to credit,
Instead of reducing, reusing and recycling.

Jesus said, "Look at the birds of the air,
They neither sow nor reap, but my father,
Feeds them. Look at the lilies of the field,
Solomon in all his glory was not dressed as one of these."

So, if we have food, clothing, a place to live,
We shouldn't want any more, but we do,
Lord, help me to spend on the things I really need,
To be thankful for those things that are truly mine.

TAEKWONDO (70)

Reflection: When my son was in the fourth and fifth grade he took karate lessons with the Young Champions of Baldwin Park. He soon gave up martial arts for the violin and Cub Scouts. In his 19th year he decided he would get fit, got on a strict diet and enrolled in a taekwondo class. He quickly moved from 110 pounds to 135. Today he will be taking his yellow belt test.

TAEKWONDO (70)

Hi kicks, round house, front kick,
Hammer fist, back fist, punch, jab,
Kia! Yes sir! Even if she is a female instructor.

A family structure, respect, dignity,
Respect of elders, responsible, on time,
Life lessons, goals, tournaments, win or lose.

Taekwondo, the art of self-defense,
Fighting against depression, disillusionment,
The ancient arts of taekkyon, takkyon and subbak,
Rivalry between the three great Korean kingdoms.

My son is lifting weights now,
Working on improving his self-image,
He is determined to improve his weight and power,
A warrior of the heart, headed for success.

Well, there is historical background for taekwondo,
But there is also a Mexican explanation,
You know why they call it taekwondo?
Porque no sabes kwondo te dan una buena patada.
You never know "cuando" (when)
You're gonna get a nice good kick. ☺

TAKE UP YOUR MAT (71)

Reflection: In the Holy Bible there is a plethora of stories
laced with hope and dreams coming true. One of these
stories is about a quadriplegic who sought Jesus' help.
When he heard that Jesus was in town the quadriplegic was
determined to receive healing. When he arrived at the
house where Jesus was, unable to enter through the door
due to mobs of people, his friends climbed a tree to the
roof, made a hole on the roof and let him down right in
front of Jesus. I think it is time for me to take up my mat
and walk in style.

TAKE UP YOUR MAT (71)

"Son, your sins are forgiven!"
"I tell you, take up your mat and go home."
The paralyzed man got up and his dream to walk,
Became a miracle right before his eyes!

Then I thought of myself,
I need to take up my mat and walk too.
I may not be a quadriplegic,
But sometimes I feel that I am stuck.

Take off your sheets and get up!
Take up your lucky pen and write!
Walk out, let your limo take you places.
Whatever you need to do, pick it up!

Let yourself down through the roof if necessary,
And bow down before the feet of Jesus.
Take up your mat, you are forgiven,
And walk through life in style! ☺

THANK YOU (72)

Moral: It is customary for many bus riders to say thank you to the bus driver as they get off the bus. Recently, I met a driver who showed all her customers courtesy by saying thank you as they got off the bus. I told her that I was a bus poet and I would dedicate a poem to her in acknowledgement of her cordial treatment of her passengers. We live in a world where consideration for others is dissipating. We need more "please and thank you" kind of people.

THANK YOU (72)

There are all kinds of people,
As there are all kinds of bus drivers.
Some are very cordial, others rude,
Others love their job, others hate it.

I boarded the bus and met up,
With a very caring woman who greeted me,
Immediately I noticed she went out of her way,
To show her appreciation for her passengers.

No matter who the passenger was,
Old, young, woman, man, poor, rich,
She said thank you to all her riders as they got off,
They replied with a thank you as well.

I began to think about those people,
Who don't show gratitude when they,
Are dropped off safely at their destination.
They don't appreciate comfort of an AC'd bus.

Now, I'd like to take the opportunity,
To say thank you to all bus drivers,
Who risk their lives daily to take us home,
Thank you, Jesus, for letting me ride this bus.

THE CHILD INSIDE (73)

Message: Children have the faith that the Bible talks about. A child can dream the impossible. Then they grow up and discover the other side of the world. If you want to accomplish great things in life you have to start dreaming again. Of course, now that we are older we realize that we have to work hard for our dreams and make them happen.

THE CHILD INSIDE (73)

Close your eyes so you can see,
Imagine you can be everything at the same time,
Release the child inside to believe, to accomplish,
Jesus said, "Let the children come to me."

So go to Jesus with your wants and desires,
Ask your Heavenly Father for the things you want,
Run like a child and don't be scared,
Imagine the father you always dreamed of.

Release the child inside, you are a child,
Your movement is not impaired, go on!
Time to engage in your best performance,
Time to go far and beyond.

So release the child inside! Leave your cares behind.
Be the pastor, sensei, the virtuoso violinist, all at the same time!
You flipped students 180 degrees, some 360 degrees, ☹
Now flip houses, write more books, stand up and have fun!

If you want to be a standup comedian, stand up and be funny!
The sky is the limit, measured only by your imagination,
Now release the child inside you and chase all your dreams.
The distance between your dreams and reality is YOU! ☺

THE FERRARI PRINCIPLE (74)

Principle: For years I have told people that the belief in God can be contrasted and compared with a Ferrari. Later the concept earned the name of The Ferrari Principle. The idea is that believing in God is more demanding than believing in material things. God requires love, commitment, obedience, etc., while a Ferrari needs only gasoline to make it run. People want all their questions answered about God but a Ferrari, they will take it for a spin in a second.

THE FERRARI PRINCIPLE (74)

If I gave you a Ferrari with the pink slip,
And convinced you it was yours no strings attached,
You wouldn't ask any questions.
You would get in, rev it up, and take off!

You would not say, now wait a minute,
How do I know this is a Ferrari?
You would not take the engine apart,
"I want to know everything there is to know."

"I want to tell you that Jesus loves you.
He wants to give you eternal life.
He is the only true God who can protect you.
I invite you to open your heart and give Him your life."

"Wait a minute now, how do you know this?
How do you know that God even exists?
What about Buddha, Mohamad, the Virgin Mary?
You can't fool me, you can't prove anything!"

The difference is that God is like us.
He needs love, appreciation, and respect.
I'm not saying you can't have a Ferrari,
Put God in your Ferrari, and you can have both.

THE MOST DANGEROUS THING (75)

Message: With all the craziness in the world today, deranged shooters, talk of nuclear war, racial unrest and much more, life can look quite bleak for your average pessimist. I continued pondering all the dangers of life and I asked myself what could be the most dangerous thing? Like an unplanned miracle it became a Facebook post and I decided to create a poem based on all the answers I received. Hope you get a taste of my humor on such a serious subject. ☺

THE MOST DANGEROUS THING (75)

What is the most dangerous thing you can do?
Is it not to love, or to love unconditionally?
Not to breathe or not getting out of bed?
Does it depend on the person, how he drives a car?
Is it those who recklessly endanger others or not being nice?
How about giving your soul to the devil or denying God?

A bit of humor: travel in Mexico or testify against Hillary,
Sin against the Holy Spirit or kill another person,
Speak words of discouragement to children,
Not to love your neighbor, lying, giving up,

Maybe being mean, doing nothing,
Meet up with a stranger 10,000 kilometers, across the Atlantic,
Think too highly of yourself, and more.
I was having so much fun that I requested Trump Dumps.

Well, here is my answer, none of the above can happen,
Unless you are alive, being born is the most dangerous thing.
You are now susceptible to all of the above and more.
The time has now come, to lay down your life,
For the man who stilled the waters and calmed the storm.
I am passing through on my way to heaven, to my Lord Jesus.

THE ORANGE MAN (76)

Principle: This poem has been revamped for the last hour.
Some friends told me that it didn't belong in this collection. It is
not my intent to be political, but instead just. Any country that
mistreats their foreigners is in the wrong. We are all humans and
we belong on this earth together. Unfortunately, I think I am
talking about a utopia that can only be possible in another
dimension, perhaps heaven.

THE ORANGE MAN (76)

The orange man is deporting,
Deporting everyone who is not from America,
I guess he never read Deuteronomy 10:17-19,
You are to love all foreigners as yourselves.

The other orange man by the freeway,
Who would rather work than beg on the streets,
Who just wants to survive, to feed his family,
He is hoping to be loved and accepted someday.

But the orange man in the White House is preparing,
ICE to deport everyone who is illegally here,
His cold heart is willing to separate parents from their children,
America is going to be great again!

The other orange man continues to sell his oranges,
He hopes to have his own fruit stand one day,
His children are US born, so he thinks they are safe,
He dreams that one day everything will be fine.

I hope the orange/white man at the will turn blue one day,
And see the harm he is causing these innocent children,
This poem may offend, it may not make any sense,
Much like the senseless bigotry ruling the earth today. ☹

THE POET TREE (77)

Reflection: This is another one of those poems that was written during a workshop at Santa Catalina Branch Library under www.saturdayafternoonpoetry.com, directed by Don Kingfisher Campbell. I have a few poems that allude to the wonder of our trees. Pondering, I imagined a tree that was a poet, obviously a take from the word "poetry". Poetry is a fountain where one can express one's feelings: sadness, anger, joy, beliefs and more. I am always amazed at the creativity of my colleagues to write about anything and everything. Therefore, if I am working on Riding the Bus with Jesus, I have to "Jesusize" my poems.

THE POET TREE (77)

Love is everywhere, it's in the air.
It's in a tree, it is in its bark, in its leaves.
If you do not have love, you are not looking.

Remember the "Giving Tree" who loved a little boy,
To the end, till he was an old man on a stump.
How about loving yourself, in a cool breeze?

Listen to the tree speak, the wind whistling,
Through its leaves telling the story of others,
Who sat under its shade, with hope and dreams.

I am the poet tree, listen to me, look and see,
Beyond what you can imagine, beyond my bark,
I love you. Should you and I die together,

My trunk, all that I am, I will give to you to build,
Your final resting place. If all that is left is my stump,
I will give it to you, my roots still in the ground,
To spring up and do it all over again.
You know, my Lord Jesus hung on one like me.

THE PRODIGAL BUS RIDER (78)

Moral: In the Bible there is a parable known as the "prodigal son".   It is a story of a son that left his father, took his inheritance and squandered it in the fast life.   When he went broke and homeless he landed a job feeding pigs, and being so hungry he was tempted to eat the slop he was feeding the pigs. He finally understood that his place was with his father and he returned to him asking for help and forgiveness.   My place is on the bus.

THE PRODIGAL BUS RIDER (78)

He rode the bus of life for three years,
And published three books of poetry,
Then the cares and challenges of life,
Overtook him, his dream lost in the abyss.

Looking back, he remembered those tranquil rides,
That allowed him to rest, sleep, write and dream,
Now he was again behind the wheel, enslaved,
A yearning desire to pick up his lucky pen and write.

Time passed and the prodigal bus rider repented,
Of the sin of neglecting his bus venue, his dream,
The dream to publish ten books,
And change the lives of his readers.

Now he is gradually going back to his riding,
His writing, his inspiring, his saving, his dreaming,
His fourth book, "Riding the Bus with Jesus"
Will be his apology, please take him back.

Nobody is perfect, everyone has gone off the path,
What is important is that you get back on track,
Looking back only to see where you tripped.
Now step up and move forward toward your dreams!

THE PRODIGAL DAD (79)

Reflection: As I said in my previous poem the story commonly known as the Prodigal Son depicts the life of a son who squandered his father's inheritance in the fast life. Much is said about the vagabond son, but little is said about the pain the father endured. For example, Rick Warren, author of the Purpose Driven Life tells about the struggles he went through when his son committed suicide. This poem is a correlation between what the father of the prodigal son might have felt as he saw his son deteriorate and what other fathers may encounter. A father needs to be strong when his son is struggling.

THE PRODIGAL DAD (79)

He stopped living,
When his son stopped dreaming,
He stopped raising cattle,
Tending his sheep.

His vineyard was dry,
And his wheat fields were barren,
It was time to be a dad again,
Ready for the rise of his son.

A father needs to remain strong,
When his son is weak,
Should the son want to return,
He will need a place to take refuge.

The prodigal dad pulled up his straps,
He replenished his storehouse,
The father thought, "I need to be ready,
With the fatted cow when my son returns.
When I see him coming afar,
I will run, kiss him and welcome him home!

THE PRODIGAL HUSBAND (80)

Moral: Seriously, I could write an infinite series of poems with the word "prodigal": the prodigal teacher, the prodigal principal, the prodigal politician, the prodigal wife…, people who are not living the life they should be living. In Riding the Bus with Jesus, you will find four: dad, poet, rider and husband. If you feel that there are areas in your life that you can improve, you can be the "prodigal you". The purpose is not to put myself down or anyone else, but actually encourage everyone to improve in anything or any role they play in life.

THE PRODIGAL HUSBAND (80)

He got lost in his career,
Hours on the freeway away from his wife,
Hours in the library doing research,
Dedicating his afternoons and weekends to his students.

Is there anything in your life that you can do better?
I challenge you to improve, to change the quality of your life,
Are you neglecting yourself, your loved ones?
Go back to the place you know you should be.

He came back to his wife to wash dishes, to clean the yard,
To water the plants, to fix wall plugs, lay down a new roof,
To fix doors, install a peep hole, fix the air conditioner,
To regenerate her heart and wake up the dormant love.

Do you need to recommit to your dream?
To love and support those dear to you?
Are you ready to meet change head-on?
Time to learn and check your resources.

I am ready to search where I belong,
With God on my side, nothing can go wrong,
How about my wife, is she ready?
Is she going to prepare for me a fatted chicken? ☺

THE PRODIGAL POET (81)

Message: Humans are social creatures. We need to belong somewhere, belong to someone. I found this poetry club in Pasadena thanks to my new-found friend, Don King-Fisher Campbell. Here, with other crazy poets I have never felt more at home. Having gone through divorce, having a suicidal son, being financially in the gutter, having difficulty at work sent me on an arduous road of depression. It was in this environment that God helped me to be more accepting of myself and circumstances. I thank God for poetry!

THE PRODIGAL POET (81)

I found the greatest group ever,
Then I abandoned my poet father,
The king that taught me how to fish.
I allowed the cares of daily life,
Draw me away from my true calling.

I got lost in grading papers,
Immersed in lesson plans no one would follow,
Being a chauffeur to my son, and his flaming violin,
Depression robbing me of my true self,
Living another life, not my own.

Then I remembered www.saturdayafternoonpoetry.com,
Like church on the Holy Sabbath,
Being encouraged and lifted up,
I was welcomed back with open arms,
Then I heard GT shout, "Kill the fatted cow!"

Now I am writing, inspiring again,
My flaming lucky pen carving on paper,
Chasing my dream, back to home base again.
All that is my Father's is mine again. ☺

THE REST IS THE BEST (82)

Moral: At Faith Community Church Pastor Jim Reeve tells us that the rest of our lives is going to be the best of our lives. Divorce, a broken relationship or a bad business deal or any other misfortune is not the end. We can start all over again and trust God all over again. Failure does not determine our character but bouncing back and learning from our mistakes molds us into the person we were meant to be. So if you look back, do it only to see where you have been, what you learned.

THE REST IS THE BEST (82)

You have fallen,
You have been slandered,
You have been cheated,
That is what happened.

What counts is what "will" happen,
You will get up stronger,
The truth will be revealed,
Justice will be served.

For God has good thoughts about you,
Plans to prosper you, to give you peace,
To give you a future and a hope,
The rest of your days will be the best.

You lost your wife, retired early,
Your children are struggling now,
But things are going to get better,
The rest of your life will be the best.

So, hang on to the hundreds of promises,
The Bible is full of great instructions for life,
There are hundreds of self-help books,
The future is yours and with God on your side...?

THE WANT TO REST (83)

Reflection: I have to say it again, I have been working since I was 10 years old. Our family came from Tijuana to work on the fields of the Central Valley. We picked tomatoes, apricots, grapes, onions, sugar beets, and other fruits and vegetables. We woke up early in the morning in freezing temperatures and by noon scalding hot and no shade. After twenty-seven years of teaching I decided it was time to change gears and dedicate myself to my other passions, for example, sleeping. ☺

THE WANT TO REST (83)

The drowsiness of my eyes,
The dread of Monday morning,
The design of lesson plans.

The call of parents and students,
The meet with the principal,
The stay awake when tired.

The can't take naps in the middle of the day,
The nod of my head at department meetings,
The facade to have everything under control.

The lost in thought,
The fear of the unknown,
The pray for a better tomorrow.

The wait for retirement,
The wonder what will happen,
The have faith, trust in the invisible.

The wait to finally rest,
No, I am not talking about death,
I am talking about sleeping,
Until your eyes fall to the back of your head. ☺

THEY GROW UP (84)

Reflection: Our children grow up so fast! By the time most us pick up the book on how to raise children, they are over 10 years old. We raise them the way we think is best but ultimately, they will choose their own path. We have to enjoy and cherish those moments when our children are small to prepare us for the next faze: to appreciate their adulthood.

THEY GROW UP (84)

And they grow up so fast, in a flash,
"Kibishti, kibishti!", my daughter, look at that!
"Muñumumuñm", McDonald's, her favorite,
"Tápate, Tápate, Tápate", when she was cold.

My son, "Chicken, chichen", I want McDonalds.
"Ia, ia", astonished by whatever he saw,
"Tisisto, tisisto", Can you change my diaper?"
"Chicup, chicup", I want some catchup, please.

Now they are all grown up,
From elegant words to profanity,
She is for Black Lives Matter and Rat's Rights,
If she keeps it up, she's gonna head a coup d'état.

My son is the quiet one,
No obscene words coming out of his mouth,
He has taken up the character of his father,
But he too blames the rich and the government.

It is so difficult to let our children go,
We want to keep them young and protected,
But I put them in Your Hands Dear Lord,
You will draw them back to You in due time.

THREE CHIPS (85)

Moral: I like to make people laugh. Laughter can bring joy to one's soul. Sometimes at the cash register I will be asked if I have a chip, and I respond, "I have three chips, one on my card and one on each shoulder." Obviously, it's a joke and I can see a smile emerging. Other frowns behind me turn into happy faces.

THREE CHIPS (85)

I walked up to the cash register,
Long faces behind me, impatient,
The cashier displayed a tired face.

"Do you have a chip on your card, sir?"
"Oh yes, definitely, one on my card,
And two more chips, one on each shoulder."

She looks at me puzzled, a little confused,
Yes, I'm hot on my right shoulder,
And awesome on my left,
Then her eyes squinted and her lips elongated.

I began to think about it,
I am hot 'cause God made me perfect,
I am awesome 'cause God loves me.

If you are ever confused about your self-worth,
Remember God made you perfect and He loves you,
Expose your three chips proudly next time,
Put a smile on your cashier's face.

Do not pass up the opportunity to bring joy,
To those tired, depressed souls you meet on your way,
A smile can alleviate a thousand woes.

THROUGH IT ALL (86)

Reflection: Life is full of challenges that shape and mold us. Remember to look at the positive side. Don't look at what you lost but look at the lesson you learned. I think I have said this before, but that's ok. Sometimes some things are worth repeating and revisiting.

THROUGH IT ALL (86)

You've gone through stuff,
But you didn't stay in it,
You had challenges but you changed,
It all ended triumphantly.

You didn't fail, you learned,
You didn't lose anything, you gained,
Your limbs were pruned, new blossoms,
Wait for the rain and sun to spring up again.

This time it's going to be better,
Last year is last year, the past,
This year is this year, a new opportunity,
Don't look back unless you are reflecting.

You went through it, you didn't stop,
But stop now to appreciate yourself,
Look at all you did, what you tried,
Now look at today and hope for tomorrow.

Thank God He brought you through it all.
Now, move forward to your future,
And get ready to go through more stuff.
Take life with a grain of salt.

TOUCH JESUS (87)

Message: The Bible passage Mark 5:25 tells the story of a woman with a continuous flow of blood. When she saw Jesus, she approached the crowd and believed she would be healed if she could only touch the hem of His garment. Later in Mark 6:56, many sick people were brought to Jesus and they believed that if only they could touch the hem of His garment, they would be healed. They probably heard what had happened to the woman.

TOUCH JESUS (87)

A woman with loss of blood from childhood,
Struggled through a crowd of people,
"If only I can touch his garment I will be healed."
Jesus turns to the woman and declares.
"Your faith has made you well."

If you want to touch Jesus for your issues,
Leaf through His pages for healing,
The Bible is full of ways you can touch Jesus,
Jesus is dressed with love, joy, peace,
Lend a helping hand and you will touch Jesus.

Everywhere Jesus went the sick followed,
And everyone struggled through the crowd,
Those who managed to touch Jesus were healed,
Struggle through the maze of life toward Jesus,
Only touch His hem and you will be healed.

Today Jesus is still dressed in truth and humility,
Touch his words, touch the skies, touch others,
Learn how Jesus is dressed through the Spirit,
Put your trust in the Omnipresent, Omni sapient,
Put on the fruits of the Spirit and be healed!

TRUST IN ME (88)

Message: I have noticed that when we pray we lay down a series of do's and don'ts for God. Then I started to think about what God would say to me, ask me to do. I think I heard him say, "Trust me". I was ready to ask Him for two wheelchairs (please read Two Wheelchairs in Riding the Bus 3) when I decided I would just trust Him. I was running and panting for a bus that never showed. An hour later the late bus arrived and all was ok.

TRUST IN ME (88)

I'm running again,
One cool Saturday morning,
Not sure if I will catch,
The weekend bus on time.

I was ready to ask God,
For two wheelchairs again,
But then I thought I heard,
A voice say, "Trust in me."

Trust in me with your wife,
Trust in me with your children,
Trust in me with your bus,
Trust in me with everything.

An hour later the bus,
Had not yet arrived at its stop,
No time wasted, I had time,
To exercise, think and pray. ☺

TWILIGHT (89)

Reflection: Today's writing seminar involved a new genre of poetry known as "erasure". We had to take a published text and circle random words on the text and then produce a new work of art. I imagined my poetry, sometime in the future, being erased on some workshop inspiring a new work of art. I made the comment that there was hope for my poetry after all, some day it will be erased. Here is my attempt to create a poem with 13 random words that I picked out of a page of a romance novel.

TWILIGHT (89)

I am in the twilight of my life,
Slowly watching myself unravel,
My past has been opened and exposed,
Like a book that tells the whole story.

Time has passed and the clock is ticking,
Sometimes I am impatient to see the end,
I want my life to sound like a boom,
Like the quake that tore the veil in half.

Now I look into the mirror that tells it all,
My life has been written for all to scrutinize,
I know now that I don't know what is to come,
My poetry has been scanned and idealized.

One thing I realize, everything repeats itself,
I have waited this long to do the impossible,
The rules of the game have been changed and broken,
Now, my fate, I fetch my lucky pen to dream again!

Finally, I sit here chuckling inside,
There is future for my poetry, one day,
It will go through the erasure process,
Edited and revamped by other minds at work.

TWO BAGS (90)

Moral: This is another poem about making people laugh. Now many stores are going green and bags are charged to encourage people to reuse bags. Bags are dropped on the floor by careless people, they go to the street drains and end up in the ocean, causing harm to our sea life. Those that make it to the landfills take years to decompose, but watch how I twist the issue of bags.

TWO BAGS (90)

Our earth is in trouble,
Technology and industrialization,
Is showing its ugly side,
The very things that the earth provides,
Are the very things that are destroying it.

Rather than looking at the bad side,
Let's play with the idea for a while,
People need to laugh and forget the issue,
To escape from reality, from the horrid side.

"Do you need a bag today sir?"
"No thank you, I always carry two bags,"
One under each eye, for emergencies."
Laughter breaks out ☺, our earth may be sick,
But one thing for sure, we are all getting older.

Meet the challenges of life with a smile,
Find the humor in getting old,
Plastic bags may contaminate the environment,
But imagine if people too were made of plastic.
Don't let the environment contaminate your soul.

UCLA (91)

Reflection: Writing poetry is an art. I am always amazed at the talent of my colleagues to turn anything into anything. In this poem I will attempt to use acronyms to show the compassion that I hope God feels when he looks at cities like Los Angeles. It is sad how we see so many homeless, poor, mentally ill people on the streets. We have to do something, we are God's hands, eyes and feet.

UCLA (91)

UCLA, UC Berkeley, UC Irvine,
UC Merced, UC Riverside, UC San Diego,
UC San Francisco, UC Santa Barbara,
UC Santa Cruz, and UC Me on this bus.

UC the rich and the poor,
UC the hearts and minds,
And what lurks within them all,
UC, I totally depend on you.

UC the benign, the malignant, the horrendous,
UC the perpetrators of violence,
UC the peace makers, the lovers of all,
UC all the souls on my limo.

UC the streets, highways and byways,
Its ups and downs, twists and turns,
UC my wife, son and daughter,
UC capitalists capitalizing on the underprivileged,

UC the invisible, past, present and future,
There is nowhere, where I can hide,
UC me as you servant, your child,
And ICU as my Lord and Savior.

UNLESS YOU... (92)

Moral: Often times I find myself talking to God, praising Him
for who He is. It is then when I realize how helpless I am
without God in my life. I think that, even if someone doesn't
believe in God, if they look down deep inside they may find an
empty spot. It is that very emptiness that faith in God can fill. I
challenge you to give God another chance.

UNLESS YOU... (92)

Unless you save me, I am not saved.
Unless you protect me, I am vulnerable.
Unless you provide, I have needs.

Unless you inspire me, I've nothing to say.
Unless you give me life, I am dead alive.
Unless you pick me up, I will stay down.

Unless you help me, there is no hope.
Unless you give me a friend, I am lonely.
Unless you give me a wife, I prefer single.

I think of all the things I have accomplished,
If you didn't educate me, no college degree,
If you didn't teach me, no Spanish, French

So, thank you Lord because I realize that unless you,
Sustain me, I cannot move forward, I'm stuck.
With you I am the little choo-choo who thinks he can.

So, if you feel like you are stuck, keep saying,
I think I can, I think I can, I think I can, until,
You climb that mountain and coast down the other side.

WE PRAYED (93)

Message: Sometimes we work hard and pray hard, but we don't get what we asked for. Sometimes we pray for someone to be healed and they recover. Other times we expect healing and things get worse, even unto death. Everything has a purpose, even Jesus asked his father to let the cup of suffering go past him. There is nothing written on this, but I imagine that even his mother prayed to have Jesus saved from crucifixion. Pastor Rick Warren's son committed suicide. There is a purpose for everything: Jesus died for the forgiveness of sins and Pastor Warren publish "The Purpose Driven Life."

WE PRAYED (93)

His daughter was born with a heart condition,
Numerous visits to the hospital, painful operations.
We prayed together for his daughter,
And God answered with a "no".
Took her little soul to rest.
Why did my daughter live?

We prayed more than once,
Why was his daughter taken?
It was a difficult day when I heard the news,
I didn't know what to say,
"You enjoyed her for six months,
You can be thankful for what some men will never have."

We don't know why God allows some things,
What is he trying to teach us?
What lesson is to be learned?
When we lose a loved one?

Someday my turn will come and,
I want to live and die with a purpose.
To leave a legacy that I was once here.

WHAT DO I DO? (94)

Lesson: Public transportation is unique. When you are in the cocoon of your car you are isolated from others. The public bus helps me to focus on the big picture, to share with others.

WHAT DO I DO? (94)

A woman boarded the bus.
Her eyes were running with tears.
Do I pray for her, offer my help?
What could possibly be wrong?

A man greeted me at the bus stop with a big smile.
I greeted him and asked him about his day.
He proceeded to tell me that his mother had just passed.
His eyes became red as he struggled to hold back the tears.

The woman, I finally worked up the courage,
To talk to her and give her encouragement.
"I feel like I went to hell and back."
"Yea, but you didn't stay there, you came back."

I offered them both, my business card,
Recommended books and Faith Community Church.
"I wish I would have died in her place."
"That's what Jesus did." Tears running down his cheeks.

You can't have this experience in a car,
Only in my long-hard-limo-classy sanctuary.
A place to meet people, pray, write poetry,
Forget about my problems, focus on helping others.

So, if you're bored, focusing on your own shortcomings,
Take 5 quarters and board the public bus.
Not that you should feel better because others are not,
But you get the opportunity to enter a different paradigm.

WHAT ELSE SHOULD I DO? (95)

Reflection: I must stress again; this book of poems is transparent. No need to hide or feel ashamed when life happens. The first few years after the divorce were very difficult. Friends would ask me, "How are you doing Luis"? I would answer, I am trusting Jesus. What else can I do? What else should I do?

WHAT ELSE SHOULD I DO? (95)

People would ask, "How are you doing?"
I would answer, "Well, my daughter,
Dropped out of college, my son is suicidal,
My wife left me, and I am trusting Jesus."

The truth was, it was very difficult for me.
Although I trusted Jesus I was plagued by depression.
I was having trouble at work and I was not happy.
My finances and living situation deplorable.

The truth is, I learned to trust in Jesus,
I trusted Him in a way like never before.
My little happy bubble had busted,
I was struggling to reinvent myself.

But really, what else could I do but to trust in Jesus?
When all seems to be lost we need somebody stronger,
We need a loving God to intercede for us, to fight,
My dream had been shattered, what else could I do,

What else should I do, but to trust in Jesus,
The Savior of my life, of all of my dreams,
If you are stuck in a world of problems and depression,
Look into Jesus, you shouldn't do anything else.

WHAT HAPPENED!? (96)

Message: This poem reminds me of the book of Ecclesiastes where the author, King Solomon, describes the vanity of life. He was the richest man ever lived with more beautiful wives and concubines than any man could imagine. Yet, at the end of it all an emptiness overwhelmed him that only God could fill. His gold and silver, possessions could not compare to something as simple as depending on God. It took a small child, my son, to bring this point home.

WHAT HAPPENED!? (96)

It can be so awesome to sit and reminisce,
Going through old pictures, looking back,
My college degree, my bachelor of arts.

Remembering my teen trip to France,
My high school years coming alive again,
Junior high, a tumultuous time in life.

We move back to grammar school,
The bullying and the talent show that saved me,
The fifth-grade hero that stood up for me.

Finally, we arrive to the toddler years,
My son was startled by a baby picture,
"Look dad, that's me!" "No son, that's me."

More intrigued than before, he looks up at me,
And exclaims, "What happened!?"
At that moment I remembered Ecclesiastes,

My pride was leveled to ground zero,
I realized I was once young, now headed for old,
One day my son would replace me, as I my father.

WHEN BIRDS DIE (97)

Reflection: Death is a subject that most of us don't like to touch upon. Yet, one hundred percent of us will have to go through the experience. Recently, I experienced the death of someone very special that I was only able to meet through WeChat a week before we were to meet in person.

WHEN BIRDS DIE (97)

When a bird dies,
All others take to the skies
Announcing one-long-lost friend.

They sing of his ventures,
The early morning's searching,
For the perfect worm to share.

When a bird dies,
Does it go to bird heaven?
Although it always lived in the sky?

Did the bird die in its nest?
Was it eaten by the neighborhood cat?
Did it crash into an electric line?

What about my Chinese friend,
Whom I never met, only had the pleasure to WeChat?
Why am I talking about the death of a bird and a human?

What is important is not how but where we go,
In heaven we will be like angels, the Bible says,
Will we share the skies with our brothers, the birds?
Will we go to a place of no pain or grief?
Where the King of Kings will evermore give us comfort?

WHO IS JESUS TO ME? (98)

Lesson: During my Monday night group Bible study our leader gave us a practical exercise to help us reflect on the identity of Jesus. I took this as an opportunity to write a quick poem on how I see Jesus. This exercise reminded me of Mark 8:29 when Jesus asked his disciples, "Who do you say that I am?" I believe that every individual needs to answer this question for himself/herself. This poem highlights some the ways I feel about Jesus, my Savior.

WHO IS JESUS TO ME? (98)

My savior from hell, from danger.
My protector from evil.
My provider of food and shelter.

My counselor, sharing my problems.
My healer when all else fails.
My future, my life in His hands.

Jesus is many things to me.
That I can't even put into words.
He has always been there for me.

My hope when I can't find the answer.
My inspiration to believe in the impossible.
My assurance that all will be well.

Therefore, Jesus is my everything.
Even those things I forgot to mention.
He knows what I will say before I speak.

He knows what I am thinking,
He is my psychologist,
He knows my next move before I do.

WHO'S BELLY (99)

Message: The Bible can be a very practical book. Its stories can be applied to everyday living. In the Old Testament you will find the story of Jonah who decided to go against God's will, His destiny. The road he took led Jonah to a ship and then the belly of a great fish. My question is: In who's belly are you hiding?

WHO'S BELLY (99)

What do you want from life?
Are you on the road to get it?
Have you swayed from your destiny?
It's ok, we all lose our way once in a while.

Have you delayed going to college?
Are you afraid to invest in real estate?
Are you willing to learn how business works?
Have you done your homework today?

In who's belly are you hiding?
Are you stuck in the belly of the monster?
Of fear, doubt, excuses, the unknown?
Turn your heart to God, your better destiny.

Look at yourself, where did you go wrong?
How can you do things better?
It's not your fault, nobody's fault,
Pick yourself up, when the fish spits you out.

And all this time, I was talking to myself.
I am the one who is hiding, I put my dreams on hold,
It is time to stop running in the wrong direction, it's time.

WHY? (100)

Message: I like this poem a lot. It is probably my favorite, but I say that about almost all my poems? This one is special because it asks the perpetual question: why? People pretend to have the answer to this question but a child's curiosity is never quenched. The truth is, I think, that what we think we know is all based on faith, evidence is worthless without faith.

WHY? (100)

Why did You die for me on the cross?
Why was I born with a sinful nature?
Why was I given the knowledge between good and evil?
Why do I have a free will to do what I want?

Why are you the only begotten Son of God?
Why are you the only way to the Father?
Why are you seated at the right hand of the Father?
Why did you send the Counselor to take your place?

Why must I love you with all my heart, soul and might?
Why did You say there is a lake of fire?
Why do other people say there is no hell?
Why do some believe there is a purgatory?

Why do some say You don't exist?
Why are there so many religions?
Why does everyone else say everyone else is wrong?
Why don't You just explain everything to us?

Why?

WORD WAR (101)

Reflection: I have continued going to my Saturday Afternoon Poetry club at Santa Catalina Branch Library in Pasadena for almost three years. We write poetry, publish, we have poetry readings, featured poets, open mic and sometimes we have critique day. Critiquing poetry may in occasions get hot. You should not attend on critique day if you don't want constructive criticism. The criticism can be so intense that your poem will completely be dismantled. In life you should listen to opinions, assess the information and then draw your own conclusions.

WORD WAR (101)

We are all sitting around a square table,
Our poems like guns loaded,
Words, thoughts and opinions flying,
Through our venue like death stars.

Everything is structured, you wait your turn,
Or the master of ceremony will chop you up!
Only one comment at a time, and then,
The free-for-all, when we can speak openly.

It's your turn, your poem on the table,
Is it good, do you like it, will they like it?
Are you ready for constructive criticism?
Will your poem improve or get destroyed?

"I don't see what is wrong,
Why should I change it?"
The fish speaks out, "If you can't take the heat,
Get out of the kitchen, you are dismissed!"

Well, this is Riding the Bus with Jesus,
So, I have to tell you what the Bible says,
"A wise man has many counselors,
Be slow to speak, quick to listen, and slow to anger."

WRITING WITH A PURPOSE (102)

Reflection: At this moment I am on my limo, Foothill line 187 on route to Santa Catalina Branch Library to teach a class titled, Writing with a Purpose. I thought the best thing I could do was to write another "bus" poem to prepare for this workshop. Recently a friend encouraged me to reflect upon myself and consider perhaps my "purpose" or reason for writing. I was fortunate to have her point that out to me and I discovered that my main purpose for writing is to share myself with others. So while I am on the bus, I am also going to attempt to have a pic taken with my fellow bus buddies. ☺

WRITING WITH A PURPOSE (102)

We all have a purpose in our life,
No matter what we are doing,
Walking, driving, writing, or riding.

What do you want to do?
Rick Warren decided he would inspire,
Especially after the death of his son.

Francis Chan paid back to the church,
All his salary, sized down, and gave more,
Just like Jesus told the rich young man.

Joel Osteen takes no money from his church,
He makes millions off of his best sellers,
Lives his life under the microscope of others.

I have discovered my purpose,
To share myself with others, to inspire, dream,
To lend a helping hand when needed.
To leave a positive mark on every person I meet.

YOU DON'T BELONG HERE (103)

Moral: Have you ever done something that was out of your character? Have you ever been somewhere you were not supposed to be? We are social beings, we are all trying to belong. Sometimes we do things we don't want to do simply because we want to be accepted. At times it may seem like you are living someone else's life, not your own.

YOU DON'T BELONG HERE (103)

He was tired of saying no to the popular crowds,
The drugs, the sex, the parties screaming at him,
Finally, he succumbed to the peer pressure,
He put the books aside to tend to the social life.

His grades began to fall, and enrolled in party school,
Now the sleepless nights turned a different color,
The depression and lack of self-esteem drowned in sparkles,
His holiness became "onliness" in free sex and the party life.

One day deep in the joy, he ran out screaming,
"The bathroom mirror told me I am good-looking!"
His self-esteem got a taste of narcissism,
For a moment he felt he could do anything.

Then the moment when things make you go, hmmm.
His friend turns to him bewildered and blurs out,
"You don't belong here, you are not one of us."
Immediately, his hairs around his ears stood straight up.

No matter what he was doing,
God was always in the back of his mind,
He then confirmed his life had to change,
Slowly he began the road to recovery.

YOU'RE GOING TO KILL HER! (104)

Moral: Sometimes wives and husbands don't agree. One has to act against the other's will. Perhaps, had he not acted with conviction his daughter would have passed. The Lord knows the past, present and future. God knew what would have happened.

YOU'RE GOING TO KILL HER! (104)

It was Christmas of 2003,
He had just bought his new house,
Everything seemed to be perfect
Just when vacation came around,
His daughter developed a high fever,
Took her to the hospital several times.
Vomit, high fever, stomach pain.

It was a tug of war,
He would take the covers off,
And she would put them back on.
He would take her to the doctor and she disagreed.
"You're going to kill her!" she reprimanded,
As long his daughter complained of pain,
He was going to take her to the hospital.

Two weeks had passed, appendicitis not defected,
By chance her regular doctor was on duty,
"If you didn't bring her in this afternoon,
She would not have made it through the night."
The doctor was furious with his staff.
"How could you not have detected appendicitis?"

With tears in her eyes, pain in her stomach,
His nine-year-old princes, "Mommy, mommy, please."
His little angel was immediately prepped for surgery,
He cried as her little body was rolled away for operation,
"Lord, save my little daughter, I love her so much." ☹

CONCLUSION

Well, now you have gone through this journey and ready to start a new one. Hopefully, you have been able to identify with my struggles and the struggles depicted through my characters. You know that they survived and you should recognize that you can survive too, but not only survive, but thrive! Let me say this: what is important is not that you went through a challenge but that you went through a challenge and didn't stay there.

Hopefully after reading my stories and poems, you came to the realization that believing and following Jesus is not easy in some ways. The world of thought, philosophy, atheism, apologetics sends so many messages that can send a person in the firm belief of nothing. I just finished watching a debate between a Christian and an atheist, titled "Why I am a Christian and why I am not a Christian." Neither side came to any general consensus, they came in disagreeing and left disagreeing. Both sides gave legitimate argument to refute the other, but they both should have agreed that "faith" is required to believe in anything. What one side called a fact, the other called a myth.

I am glad that I didn't set out to prove anything in my poems. I shared myself earnestly with you with no strings attached. Ultimately everyone choses to believe what they want to regardless of what others say and they will embrace whatever makes sense to them. I believe in Jesus because I chose to, not because of what others told me to believe. I believe in Jesus in and of myself. I did not discuss, heaven, hell, whether there are three heavens, a purgatory or whether Jesus is a God or a prophet. Theology and debate were not the purpose of my poems. I do hope nevertheless that you will give Jesus a chance and search out answers for yourself, as I have. Jesus said, "Seek and You shall find." So, if you are looking for something, you will find it. ☺

Made in the USA
Las Vegas, NV
24 December 2023

83128088R00079